CREATIVITY
FOR KIDS

Dear Colton and Lana,

Merry Christmas! I sure love you two a lot. You know your creative Aunt Anna enjoys playing with you and using our minds to come up with fun games and things to do.

I found this book and thought my creative kiddos would LOVE fun activities that you can do with eachother, by yourself, or with an adult—there are many options! And a TON of fun, creative activities you can do.

I hope we will pick out a few to do together some time soon. You are amazing beautiful people.

Love + Merry Christmas 2020

Aunt Anna

CREATIVITY FOR KIDS

75 Fun Activities to Promote Creative Thinking and Self Expression

For Kids Ages 6 to 9

TRISHA RICHÉ

Illustrations by Aaron Cushley

**ROCKRIDGE
PRESS**

For general information on our other products and services or to obtain technical support, please contact our Customer Care Department within the United States at (866) 744-2665, or outside the United States at (510) 253-0500.

Rockridge Press publishes its books in a variety of electronic and print formats. Some content that appears in print may not be available in electronic books, and vice versa.

Interior and Cover Designer: Suzanne LaGasa
Art Producer: Janice Ackerman
Editor: Shannon Criss
Production Editor: Emily Sheehan

Cover and Interior Custom Illustration: © 2019 Aaron Cushley

ISBN: Print 978-1-64611-192-3 | eBook 978-1-64611-193-0

R0

This book is dedicated to my eclectic tribe of friends and family. Each of you adds vibrant color to my world. Always live your dash to the fullest!

In memory of my grandmother
who lived her dash with love, honesty, and joy.

Shirley Ann Jeansonne
3/7/1940–11/23/2019

CONTENTS

INTRODUCTION

Hello, all! My name is Trisha Riché. I have always been a little quirky and eclectic and liked creating my own path. This was solidified with my exposure to so many creative outlets at the Douglas Anderson School of the Arts. I've always liked to color outside the lines and think outside the box, not to be rebellious, but to find my own way.

Since I was little, I have wanted to teach. I have wanted to inspire others to love themselves and show their weird to the world. It's good for kids and adults alike to make mistakes, show emotions, and improvise daily. As a teacher, I encourage the whole child. I show my quirks and imperfections and want kids to show theirs, too. I encourage them to try new things, make messes (yes, really!), and have fun while learning. I am totally open to new ideas and discourage any form of criticism. This makes my connections with the children genuine and their environment a safe place in which to express themselves. For all the messes and trials and errors, the reward is that I get a front row seat to watch my students grow and blossom just by being able to express themselves creatively. Children become huge risk takers (in a good way!) and get creative with their thinking because they feel safe around me.

Creative outlets like the arts help students become more confident, which often leads to academic success because they have less of a fear of failure. When you have no fear of failure, you aren't afraid to run toward new ideas and uncertainty as they are the key to creative growth. Having taught and tutored students in arts and academics for 15 years, I've witnessed this phenomenon firsthand. Parents tell me that their children have grown into their true selves and now grasp new ideas due to my hands-on, whole-child approach.

As an educator, I'm always striving to strengthen my knowledge of creativity. I continue to learn and share my findings. I presented a class on harnessing creative ideas in the classroom at a national educators' conference. My love of creativity and children drives me. A parent of one of my students nominated me for the Great American Teach-Off in 2011, and I'll never forget her words: "Her room is the one that looks like an art box exploded, and unless you know where her door is you may miss it because of the extensive decorations she uses in the hallway!"

She offered that truth, but she also explained that I make learning fun and bring it to life. Many of the students I've taught have needed interventions, but this isn't really an obstacle to me. Every child has the ability to create and learn and grow. Oftentimes it's the child who is struggling that responds best to the opportunity to create! The key is to make it fun and engaging.

In the words of author Ray Bradbury, "We have to continually be jumping off cliffs and developing our wings on the way down." Visual statement, right? He was, after all, Bradbury! It's important to allow children (and ourselves) to take risks, try new things, create, explore, think divergently, and implement different solutions. Creativity is a vital part of this process. Creativity allows us to try and to grow, and it allows our world to change and evolve for the better. Without change, the world would be stagnant.

The best thing we can do to help build our children's creative mindset is to encourage creativity from a young age. Creativity is a natural thing to children— it reveals itself as showing curiosity, asking lots of questions, and demonstrating the need to express themselves in a multitude of ways. As a caregiver or teacher, you can support their desire by providing open-ended activities and questions (those that invite expression rather than just yes or no answers), allowing choices whenever possible, and integrating multiple learning styles into activities. This way, they can explore many types of learning, and, if you watch, you'll be able to identify which way they learn best. They may also be attracted to certain aspects of creative activities.

Another way to foster creativity is to nurture their creative choices and provide a "judgment-free zone" where children, particularly younger children, feel safe to explore ideas freely. Since caregivers or teachers will likely be doing the activities in this book with them or guiding them along the way, take this opportunity to provide encouragement as they go—support their efforts and cheer on their achievements! Some children may require little to no guidance depending on their skill and age level.

No matter the age or skill level, every child has unique talents and interests. By providing creative outlets like the activities in this book, we are doing much more than keeping them busy. We're helping children sprout the seeds of growth that will make them capable, confident, analytical, problem-solving, thoughtful, insightful, team-playing game changers for the world to come!

Chapter One

What Is Creativity?

When someone instructs you to "get creative," what exactly do they mean? Like many, I once thought creativity was just "being artsy." Many people assume that you're either born with the ability to be creative or you're not. In art school, I came to realize that a lot more goes into being creative than just rapt enthusiasm for the arts. Yes, an appreciation for the arts is a part of creativity, but it doesn't embrace the entire concept. Creativity is a way of thinking of things in a new or inventive way. It's about being innovative and able to improvise when something doesn't go as planned. Creativity is an act that has been scientifically proven to promote deeper thinking, imagination, and brain development. Contrary to popular belief, creativity can be cultivated, nurtured, and grown, especially if you start at a young age. Anyone can learn to be a creative person with the right mindset. Start by trying new things, then find an interest and run with it. That's where choices come in. Ask your child if they would rather play with play dough or paint. Would they like to dance or sing? They will let you know where their passions lie!

INSIDE THE MIND OF THE CREATIVE KID

Every child's experience and path to creativity will be different. We all think and come up with different ideas in unique ways. If a child feels comfortable and valued, they will express themselves more easily because they know that their expression will be received with encouragement.

Healthy creative-expression habits that are found particularly in kids ages six to nine could include:

* Demonstrating curiosity and desire to explore ideas, especially new ones

* Expressing interest in certain subjects or objects

* Questioning the world around them

* Singing, dancing, painting, creating, and playing freely

* Expressing their feelings calmly and clearly

* Thinking deeply while problem-solving

Every child is different and may not respond to activities and conversations in the same way—that's okay! Be patient and positive, and creativity will come. Some kids may take longer than others to express their creativity on their own, especially when it comes to problem-solving.

Reducing Screen Time: Why It Matters

Studies show too much screen time can lead to developmental issues, especially in young children. It's important to limit the use of TVs, tablets, and other electronic devices to a consistently low amount of time each day, which will vary from child to child.

You may be wondering how this affects children. According to the Mayo Clinic, too much screen time is associated with:

- Weight issues
- Disrupted sleep patterns
- Behavioral issues
- Compromised social skills
- Violence
- Less playtime

From a brainpower and creativity standpoint, overexposure to electronics restricts critical thinking and problem-solving skills because of the shortage of human interaction caused by excessive screen time. This results in decreased opportunities for kids to express their ideas or feelings.

Having conversations and developing ideas are vital to cognitive development. Without plenty of screen-free occasions, social and communication skills will become weaker, and ultimately, a child's skills will regress instead of progress. You may consider television to be an opportunity for children to experience lots of communication, but in fact when watching TV, children are exposed to about one-fifth the amount of words and interactions than children who have limited screen time and more opportunities to interact with their peers and adults. The research is clear: Opting for real-life activities and interactions will help your child thrive!

THE CREATIVE PROCESS

Children are able to express creativity at a very young age. Even a two-year-old can express creativity if given the opportunity. In a child's mind, creativity is being able to use their imagination to create things. When they feel like they are able to express ideas and thoughts freely, their creativity becomes more fluid, occuring more frequently and more spontaneously.

There are five stages of a creative process:

Prepare

Incubate

Illuminate

Evaluate

Implement

First, a child thinks of or is presented with an idea or situation. Next, they begin to think about it and come up with an idea of how to proceed with actions. Finally, they take action and put their creativity into motion. This process is how inventors are born!

Guided Creativity

Creativity doesn't always come easy. Sometimes it takes a little help from others to guide children along the right path to get those creative juices flowing.

Helpful tips:

- Identify their interests. Recognizing children's interests will allow them to express their creativity more easily.

- Give children a choice. Allowing a child to decide between two options for an activity will show them that their opinion is valuable. You can then ask them why they chose that option.

- Ask guiding questions. Try questions like "What can we do next?" and "Is there another way to do this?"

- Let them make mistakes. Mistakes are proof that they are learning and growing. Sometimes I make mistakes in my classroom on purpose! It's a way to model problem-solving.

- Join in. Activities are much more fun when you do them together!

THE ROLE OF CREATIVE PLAY

Creative play is important for building imaginative skills and increasing cognitive development. Ideally, you'll want to begin integrating creative play at a young age so children can learn all the skills that come from creativity. It's so much more than play; a child who can use their imagination will always have a ready playmate.

Creative play has an important role in the following areas:

Executive Function

Executive function is the process of making decisions using a group of skills originating from the frontal lobe of the brain. Memory, flexibility, and inhibition control are a few of these crucial skills. Executive function is developed through open-ended, creative exploration in which children feel free to make mistakes and try again. Rather than seeing mistakes as a failure, they see them as a first attempt in learning. Children develop quality executive function skills by interacting with others and by learning to self-regulate reactions to situations.

Executive function allows a child to try different ways of performing tasks through individual expression and exploration. Children will learn to override their inhibitions and try new things. This will help them become risk takers and problem solvers. Instead of freezing when faced with a challenge, executive function gives children the ability to attack it head-on. When plan A doesn't go as planned, they're more inclined to try plans B to Z. Children with solid executive function skills are also more flexible when performing activities and don't feel like they must stick to a single idea. This is because their thinking has become more open, and their thought process, instead of being rigid, is able to explore new ideas and activities. These skills help their brains develop properly and lead to good memory development.

Several signs may identify that executive skills are lacking:

- ★ The child avoids trying new things or new ways of doing something.

- ★ The child does not freely express their thoughts and ideas.

- ★ The child is not able to be flexible with outcomes.

Creative play improves executive function by allowing children to make decisions and work through problems in a more constructive way, which also supports brain development and learning, once again proving that creative play is much more than just play!

Social Skills

Creative play allows children to interact with others in a cooperative way. It teaches them how to converse and work with both peers and adults. It also presents opportunities to take turns and organize ideas and activities with others. Social skills are important, as we adults know: We use them throughout our lives. When a young child lacks social skills, it can negatively impact how they react to situations. The earlier and more often children have the chance to socialize through play, the more exercise their social skills muscles will receive.

Individuality

Individuality is about honoring the unique personality in each of us and letting that uniqueness shine. It needs to be developed, as it does not come naturally. We can help with this! By being advocates for our child's unique style, we send the message that their individuality is a good thing, something to treasure and cultivate. Play is a great way to promote and grow individuality, as it affords children the chance to move, draw, create, etc., all in their own way. Individuality builds confidence—it's what makes us special—and as such, it should be celebrated in every possible situation.

Sensory Exploration and Motor Skills

Fine and gross motor skills both play important roles, and kids need to practice them often for proper development and overall well-being. Gross motor skills like jumping, running, and climbing can be practiced easily through creative pursuits in dance or dramatic play. Fine motor skills require and build hand-eye coordination. Activities such as cutting, stringing beads, and manipulating objects all lend themselves to the development of fine motor skills through creative play with STEAM (science, technology, engineering, art, and math) activities.

Vocabulary/Language

It's easy to see the value in communication, but did you know that, in addition to its obvious function as a tool for speaking, listening, reading, and writing, communication also strengthens the brain? When children can express their ideas freely through play, this helps build their working vocabulary. Creative play helps them explore and identify their likes and dislikes and form their own opinions, which they can then articulate. Creative play improves language skills and develops a broader range of ideas, creating stronger connections in the brain.

Creative Affirmations

We all need praise. For children, praise is especially vital as it affirms what they are doing is worthwhile. It also encourages them to create freely with confidence.

Here are several examples of affirmations you can build on:

- "I love the way you moved to the beat of the music!"
- "It's beautiful the way you mixed those colors on your paper to create new colors."
- "It's so clever how you built a large tower on your own."
- "You should be very proud of the way you worked through that problem and tried again."

These types of specific affirmations allow the child to see that their choices and creativity are valued. When kids feel valued, they gain self-confidence. This confidence allows them to explore even more creative avenues without fear of failure or rejection.

THE VALUE OF CREATIVITY

Creativity can be fun, but that's not its only purpose. If creative outlets didn't exist, we wouldn't have music, buildings, art, or even sticky notes! Creativity is an integral part of our society. Without it, our growth would be stagnant. Growth in our brains and society would end. Nothing would change or adapt to become better or more useful in our society. You may ask, how does this relate to children? Well, guess what? The ice pop, the trampoline, and the Braille system were all invented by children, and as society has progressed, innovators and entrepreneurs have become younger and younger. They aren't just running lemonade stands. Children are finding innovative ways to solve problems and presenting them to society in order to make the world a better place. They're creating prototypes and products, all because they were allowed to explore their ideas in creative ways starting at a very young age.

Emotional Health

Just like adults, children must be allowed to express their ideas, thoughts, and desires through different creative activities. Creative outlets help children develop into confident and emotionally sound individuals. Creativity gives children a way to express themselves in a constructive and productive way. Creative play with artwork, sand, dolls, or puppets is used in therapy to provide a window into the child's mind—a testament to the power of creative play as it relates to emotions.

Self-Expression

Creativity allows your child to express things they would like to tell or show you in a multifaceted way. The ways children can fine-tune their individuality are endless. Some become so skilled in one aspect of creativity that they choose to pursue it as a career when they become adults. Foster it! Encourage it! If your child loves photography, encourage them to enter a picture into a contest. Self-expression, and your support of it, gives your child direction as well as a sense of worth.

ENCOURAGING CREATIVITY IN KIDS

Creativity doesn't always come naturally for children, but it can be encouraged and fostered by a teacher, caregiver, or another adult they admire. When this encouragement comes from a person a child trusts, they become more comfortable getting into a creative headspace. The following tips are great ways to encourage kids toward creativity and to try something new:

Set a Time to Create

Set aside a time, at least two to three times a week, to create things with children. Mark your calendar. Kids love knowing that they will have quality time with you!

Designate a Space to Create

Have a space where they can create their ideas. It can be a special room, a section of the countertop, or even a corner set up with supplies.

Avoid Judgment

Though figuratively (and literally) speaking, they may color outside the lines, resist the urge to judge. Let your child express their ideas without telling them that what they think is wrong. They may be less likely to share their ideas in the future if you judge their thought process or actions negatively.

Growth Mindset

Sometimes, even as adults, our first instinct is to say, "I can't do it" or "I don't know how." Unfortunately, this is a learned behavior known as a fixed mindset. Conversely, a growth mindset is a way you can train your brain to look at things differently. This requires you to be flexible and responsive when things don't work as planned. A growth mindset gives you the ability to keep your thought process open and maintain a positive attitude. Encourage your child to use a growth mindset when they try new things. You can do this by teaching them to believe in themselves and by letting them know that they are always learning and growing. Offer them phrases like "We don't know how to do this yet, but let's train our brain to learn how." and "It's okay if we make mistakes. We will laugh and try again until we get it!"

Focus on Their Interests

To start off, concentrate on things you know they will like. This way they will be more open to exploring in different, creative ways.

Use Common Items

Try creating something new with items like toilet paper rolls, food and drink containers, and of course, the timeless classic—large boxes. Recycling items is a fun and worthwhile way to create.

Chapter Two

Let's Create: Imagination!

Imagination allows for creative exploration of the world around us. It promotes change and evolution by encouraging us to think of new things and create freely. Children are born imaginative and can start expressing their creativity as early as 18 months. Problem-solving, storytelling, and creative writing are just a few ways children can learn to express themselves and expand their imagination.

PROBLEM-SOLVING

Problem-solving skills are among the best tools we can have. They allow us to solve the challenges that come our way in life—and who doesn't want to be able to solve their own problems? It's much better than standing around saying, "I'm stuck!"

In addition to their obvious benefits, problem-solving skills have been proven to sharpen our memory and brain function. So, how can we develop these? By finding creative ways to do things. When children develop and practice creative problem-solving skills, whether through puzzles, experiments, or any other creative pursuit, they are learning how to navigate obstacles more easily. With practice, children also become more flexible with responses and more willing to try different ways to do things. A child's first reaction to problem-solving will soon become critical thinking and strategizing on what will work and why. Obstacles, instead of having a negative connotation, become opportunities to try something new and different. It's all about changing the "I'm stuck" fixed mindset to a "How can we fix this?" growth mindset. Without creative thinking, this shift in attitude and perception would not be possible.

Toothpick Towers (20)

Egg Drop (22)

Automaker Adventure (24)

I'm a Horse of Course! (26)

Bridge-Building Challenge (27)

Toothpick Towers

This activity is great for children who like to stack their toys and build tall towers with their blocks and Legos. Building with small materials helps develop fine motor skills. It also allows children to think critically about what their next move should be. Critical-thinking skills are an important part of learning to adapt and approach things in a creative way. And learning what steps to take to rebuild if it comes tumbling down is important, too!

Prep: None

Activity time: 30 minutes

Place: Anywhere at a solid work surface

MATERIALS

A bag of mini marshmallows

A package of toothpicks

Ruler or yardstick

STEPS

1. Direct the child to build a tower as high as they can using only mini marshmallows and toothpicks.

2. As they build, encourage them to keep going. If you notice the child struggling, you can guide them by helping with the base of the tower.

3. When they are finished with the tower, or after 15 minutes, measure the height with a ruler or yardstick.

4. Have the child count the number of toothpicks and marshmallows they used.

5. Next, challenge them to build a larger tower using the same number of toothpicks and marshmallows.

Modifications: For older or more skilled kids, challenge them to make the tower reach a certain height. You can also limit the number of toothpicks and marshmallows they can use.

For younger kids, open the bag of marshmallows and let the marshmallows sit out for a day or so to make them sturdier to work with. Get creative! You can use any candy, like gumdrops, candy corn pumpkins, or dot candies, to make this activity more fun and colorful.

Egg Drop

Does your child like to investigate how things work and try lots of different ways to do something? Curious children (and even some adults!) love the idea of dropping objects from a high place and seeing what results from it. It's a fun experiment for all!

Prep: 5 minutes

Activity time: 20 to 30 minutes

Place: Inside on a hard surface like a countertop, or outside on a hard surface like a sidewalk

MATERIALS

Packing materials such as paper towel, wash rag, bubble wrap, tissue paper

A carton of eggs

A couple of small containers for the eggs (small plastic butter containers, or something of similar size)

Tape

STEPS

1. Tell your child that you are going to investigate which material protects the egg best when dropped from 5 feet up.

2. Offer the child a variety of packing materials. Have them choose the material they feel will best protect the egg. Ask them why they think that material is the best.

3. Have them wrap that material around the egg however they'd like.

4. Next, have them place the wrapped egg in the container and tape the lid shut.

5. Drop the container from 5 feet up. Younger children may need a step stool to do this.

6. Open the container and, together, observe what happened with the egg.

7. Repeat with a new egg for each container until all eggs, materials, and containers have been tested.

8. Invite your child to share their thoughts on which material offered the best protection based on their observations and how they could tell. For example, are some eggs just slightly cracked while others are smashed?

Did you know? Children learn through curiosity, trials, and experimentation. Let the child figure out for themselves which materials work best without telling them something won't work. For example, they may believe that a tissue will totally protect that egg. Let them see the results for themselves!

Tip: Don't like to waste food? If you can, retrieve the gooey egg, fish out the shells and scramble the eggs up for the dog in your life!

Automaker Adventure

Children who like to build and create items will enjoy this challenge. Here you'll allow a child to build a car out of random recycled items. Let them get as inventive as they want with their creation—only using the items you give them!

Prep: 5 minutes

Activity time: 20 to 30 minutes

Place: Indoors at a solid work surface

MATERIALS

Food containers in various sizes (cereal box, butter container, etc.)

Soda cans, or other cans (see Safety Tip)

Caps from milk, water, or soda bottles

Straws

Tape

Glue

Markers

STEPS

1. Tell your child that they are going to build a car using only the materials provided.

2. You can guide them by asking questions like "What parts do you need to make a car (wheels, body, seats, etc.)?" or "What will you add to your car to make it special?"

3. Allow them to put their car together however they like. There is no wrong process. It's all about creativity and problem-solving! If they add something you don't recognize as a car part, ask them what it is. They may have come up with imaginative options, like a time travel feature!

Modification: For older children, have them create a futuristic vehicle and write a story about what their vehicle can do that regular vehicles can't.

SAFETY TIP: Make sure the cans are free of any sharp edges.

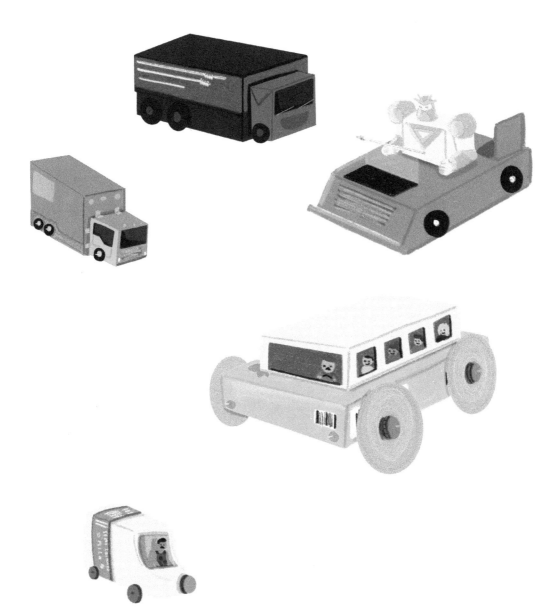

I'm a Horse of Course!

This activity presents a fun opportunity for children who love to use their imagination, have imaginary friends, or play make-believe all the time. I'm a Horse of Course helps them think of creative solutions to the problem of having different legs and needing to maneuver through life in a new way.

Prep: 5 minutes

Activity time: 20 to 30 minutes

Place: Indoors on a hard work surface

MATERIALS

Paper (optional)

Pencil (optional)

STEPS

1. Have your child draw a picture of a horse with the child's face.

2. Read them the following message: "What would you do if you woke up with the legs of a horse? Four of them! How will you get around and make it work for you?"

3. Have them look at their picture of the horse with their face on it as inspiration.

4. Encourage them to tell the story of their day. Ask them guided questions: "How would your day change because you have horse legs? Would anything stay the same? How would you deal with having to walk differently?" Use a story jar, if needed (page 30).

Did you know? Activities in which children are asked to imagine a change like this teaches them how to improvise and problem-solve quickly. When they encounter real problems, they will be more prepared and better able to cope!

Bridge-Building Challenge

How do engineers and architects get their start? By building things as kids! Building bridges is a wonderful way for children to brainstorm ideas and try multiple solutions to a problem. Set them on their way with a few easy materials; you never know where these early engineering skills will take them!

Prep: 5 minutes

Activity time: 40 minutes

Place: Indoors or outdoors at a solid work surface

MATERIALS

Paper and pencil or small container of water

Pipe cleaners

Popsicle sticks

Scotch, duct, or packing tape

2 gummy bears or small plastic figures

STEPS

1. Place the small container of water on the table or draw water on paper.

2. Place the gummy bears or figures on opposite sides of the water.

3. Read these directions to your child: "We have a problem! Mr. and Mrs. Gummy Bear are stuck on opposite sides of the water. They can't get in the water because they will melt. You have to help them by building a bridge so they can cross the water to be with each other. You can only use the materials in front of you to build the bridge. You have 30 minutes to save them. Hurry!"

4. Let your child work with the pipe cleaners, Popsicle sticks, and tape to create a bridge. They can use the paper to plan if they want to, but jumping in and using trial and error will yield greater results.

Modification: This is a high-level problem-solving activity. Younger children may need guidance to keep trying. Use guided questions such as: "What else could you add?" or "Which materials do you think will make the best bridge?" For older or more skilled children, you can increase the size of the body of water, requiring a lot more building and fancy thinking.

Did you know? Architectural structures like bridges are a form of 3-D art!

STORYTELLING

Communication skills are critical tools for all areas of life, including social, academic, and even emotional well-being. Development of these skills at a young age helps children become well-rounded and allows them to navigate life's twists and turns with a little more ease. Storytelling is a wonderful way to build these skills; in fact, by allowing your child to tell the story, you benefit even more. Storytelling increases a child's vocabulary and language skills. It stands to reason that communication becomes clearer and more fluid when a child is given opportunities to vocalize their thoughts and ideas. Storytelling also takes—and builds—confidence, imagination, and on-the-spot thinking. If it helps them be more comfortable, children can use a puppet to tell their stories. With practice, and by being the storyteller, your child will gain awesome skills. After all, they are commanding an audience with their tale!

Story Chain

This twist on the old game of Telephone takes sentences created by you and your child and puts them together to form a story. Your child will get to exercise their brain by remembering the previous sentences and creating new sentences to add on to.

Prep: None

Activity time: 10 minutes

Place: Any quiet place

MATERIALS

2 or more people

STEPS

1. Explain to your child that you will be doing a story chain, so get their imagination ready!

2. Start the story with a sentence. Have them repeat that sentence and follow it with a sentence of their own.

3. Create a story chain, by going back and forth, until you have done 8 to 10 sentences in total.

Tip: Need some suggestions for story topics? Try a family vacation, a trip to the farm, the day a unicorn magically appeared in their classroom, or when aliens came to Earth.

Did you know? Story games like this help increase a child's memory capacity by retelling after listening carefully.

What Happened Next? A Story Jar Activity

This one's for children who like to tell stories or make things up. What Happened Next? is all about thinking creatively and keeping your storytelling child on their toes, in this case by using a story jar. They will be curious to see what object they'll be incorporating into their story next!

Prep: 10 minutes

Activity time: 15 to 20 minutes

Place: Anywhere

MATERIALS

Jar containing pictures of objects, things, people, or places

STEPS

1. Tell your child that they are going to tell you a story about what happened at school today using a picture from the jar. For example, if you pull out a picture of a dinosaur, your child will need to tell you what happened in their day that involved a dinosaur!

2. Invite them to start telling the story and let them know that every time you put your hand up, they have to pick a new picture out of the jar.

3. Have them incorporate the pictured object into the next part of their story.

4. Continue this process until they have pulled 6 to 10 pictures.

Tip: Exercise your own imagination: What scenarios can you offer your child to tell a story about? Consider anything from your upcoming vacation to things you saw at the supermarket.

Did you know? This story jar strategy will help children improvise and think on their feet. It will also improve problem-solving and language skills.

Into the Future

This activity is great for children who love to use their imagination. They can choose to create any scenario they'd like—after all, it is the future, so nothing can be too outrageous. Let them predict!

Prep: None

Activity time: 10 minutes

Place: Anywhere (at a solid work surface, if incorporating writing)

MATERIALS

Story jar, if needed (page 30)

STEPS

1. Read this scenario to your child: "Tell me a story about what would happen if you traveled to the future. Tell me about all the cool new inventions you would see."

2. You can prompt them by asking: "What do people look like?" "What kind of cars do you see?" "Can cars fly?" and "What do the houses look like?"

3. Invite them to use the story jar, if needed.

Modification: For older or more skilled children, invite them to write the story and draw illustrations. Later, they can read it to you. (This will add 15 to 20 minutes to the activity time.)

Did you know? Asking children questions helps them share details and increases their vocabulary and language skills. Plus, it builds confidence as they see you're interested in what they have to say!

Cut-Out Story

Some children enjoy having visuals to help prompt a story or event. Old magazine or calendar pictures can provide endless story options to dream up!

Prep: 5 minutes

Activity time: 10 to 15 minutes

Place: Anywhere

MATERIALS

Pictures cut out from magazines or expired calendars, or calendars from the dollar store

STEPS

1. Have your child turn all the pictures facedown and mix them up.

2. Tell them they are going to tell a story about the picture they pick up. For example, if they pick a picture of a lake, they can tell a story about a day on the beach.

Modification: For older or more skilled children, you can add to the challenge. Add something to the picture from your imagination or the story jar (page 30), like a dog or umbrella. They must incorporate that object into the story they are telling.

Kingdom Ruler

Nearly all children have grand ideas of what they want to become, and children with budding leadership skills love making up rules for others. In this activity, your child will pretend to be a king or queen for the day, and they'll be able to create rules for the entire kingdom!

Prep: None

Activity time: 10 minutes

Place: Indoors or outdoors

MATERIALS

Story jar, if needed (page 30)

STEPS

1. Invite your child to tell you a story about what would happen if they became queen or king for a day.

2. Ask them guided questions like "What new rules would you make?" "How would you dress?" or "What would you have people do?"

3. You can use the story jar if they need more ideas.

Modification: For older children, discuss rules and why they are important. Then, you can discuss why they thought the rules they chose were important. Invite them to write the rules of their kingdom on a piece of paper.

Did you know? Rules give structure. They don't hinder or limit creativity. Critical thinking becomes key when working within set parameters.

WRITING PROMPTS

Writing is another great way to help improve vocabulary, language, and fine motor skills. In this section we'll use writing prompts to help your child get their creative juices flowing; these prompts give the child a starting point for an idea. Children can use their imagination to help build on that idea and create a whole story. Children become more comfortable exploring new ideas as they are given more opportunities to write creatively. There are no boundaries in creative writing. It's all about imagination in its simplest form. Their confidence will skyrocket as they learn to let their creative ideas flow onto paper. So, let's get started!

Get Home from Mars

This activity is particularly fun for children who love outer space! Here they'll explore what would happen if their space vehicle broke down on Mars. It will take some creative brain power to figure out how they will get back to Earth with only the three random items picked out of the jar.

Prep: 10 minutes

Activity time: 15 to 30 minutes

Place: Indoors or outdoors at a solid work surface

MATERIALS

Story jar (page 30) or container with random pictures your child drew

Pencil

Writing paper, preferably one with lines on the bottom and space for a picture on top. (You can print this online for free. See Resources section.)

STEPS

1. Have the child pick three pictures out of the jar.

2. Next, read the following prompt: "You are stuck alone on planet Mars with only the three objects you just picked out of the jar. Write a story about how you'll use those three items to get you safely back home to Earth."

3. Stories can be between 50 and 150 words or even longer if desired, depending on the child's age and abilities.

4. Invite your child to create pictures at the top of the page that go with their story.

Tip: You can use a story jar like this for any of the writing prompts, especially for younger kids who may need some guidance.

Shipwreck Adventure

This prompt will get your child thinking up inventive ways to survive on a deserted island alone. You may need to provide some definitions and pictures for the child if they don't know what "island," "deserted," or "stranded" mean. Let them come up with an awesome story about what they would do if they were stuck on the island.

Prep: None

Activity time: 15 to 30 minutes

Place: Indoors or outdoors at a solid work surface

MATERIALS

Writing paper

Pencil

Story jar, if needed (page 30)

STEPS

1. Read the following prompt to the child: "Your boat crashed, and you are now stranded on a deserted island. Look around—what do you see? Write a story about how you'll survive. Talk about some items from your boat that washed up on shore to help you survive until you get rescued. Did you try to get off the island?"

2. Stories can be between 50 and 150 words or longer, depending on the child's age and abilities.

3. Invite your child to create pictures that go with their story.

Zoo Escape!

Does your child love animals? This one is all about animals that break out of the zoo and run amok through the town. Your child can create any crazy events they would like to happen. Anything goes in this chaotic prompt, so watch out for the stampede!

Prep: None

Activity time: 15 to 30 minutes

Place: Indoors or outdoors at a solid work surface

MATERIALS

Writing paper

Pencil

Story jar, if needed (page 30)

STEPS

1. Read the following prompt to the child: "Somebody left the gates open at the zoo! Write a story about what would happen if all the animals escaped."

2. You can expand on the idea by prompting them: "What happened next?" "What animals did you see?" "What were they doing?" "Did they all make it back to the zoo?" and "How, why, or why not?"

3. Stories can be between 50 and 150 words or longer, depending on the child's age and abilities.

4. Invite your child to create pictures at the top of the page that go with the story.

Tip: Help your child with the details. For example, you may ask what noises the animals would be making or whether they're running on two legs or four. Do they run or gallop? What do you think that animal might want to eat in town?

Tooth Fairy Fiasco

Even the Tooth Fairy must occasionally problem-solve! This writing prompt will conjure magical and fun images as your child thinks of creative gifts the Tooth Fairy could leave under the pillow instead of money.

Prep: None

Activity time: 15 to 30 minutes

Place: Indoors or outdoors at a solid work surface

MATERIALS

Writing paper

Pencil

Story jar, if needed (page 30)

STEPS

1. Read the following prompt to the child: "Oh no! The Tooth Fairy ran out of money to give kids. Write a story about what the Tooth Fairy is putting under kids' pillows instead."

2. You can guide them by asking: "What kinds of things would you love to find under your pillow?" or "What things would surprise you or gross you out?"

3. Stories can be between 50 and 150 words or longer, depending on the child's age and abilities.

4. Invite your child to create pictures that go with their story.

Tip: You can do this prompt with the Easter Bunny, Santa Claus, or any other main character you can think of—make one up if you like!

What's Under My Bed?

What's under your child's bed doesn't need to be a scary thing! Here's a creative way to put a positive spin on scary things under the bed. It can be a lot of things, just one thing, or an entire land!

Prep: None

Activity time: 15 to 30 minutes

Place: Indoors or outdoors with a flat surface, like a table

MATERIALS

Writing paper

Pencil

Story jar, if needed (page 30)

STEPS

1. Read the following prompt to your child: "There is nothing scary under your bed. Instead there's a _____. Fill in the blank with an animal or thing that you'd love to find under your bed. Write a story about what's under your bed and how it helps you."

2. You can give an example if needed, such as a unicorn that does your homework or a puppy that finds all your lost items.

3. Stories can be between 50 and 150 words or longer, depending on the child's age and abilities.

4. Invite your child to create pictures at the top that go with their story.

Did you know? This is a creative way to help children feel safe at bedtime.

Chapter Three

Let's Create: Art!

This chapter will focus on sensory arts: drawing, painting, crafts, music, and movement/dance activities. All of these areas help get creative juices flowing and are critical to brain development. Creativity opens your child's brain to more possibilities and allows for flexibility in a given situation. Their ability to learn and academic capacity also increase. Studies show that creativity can aid blood flow to the brain and even increase life expectancy. Who knew that fun could be so good for you?

VISUAL ARTS

Have you ever heard someone say a piece of art made them "feel" something? Drawing, painting, and other visual arts have been proven to increase serotonin levels in your body, improving your mood and attitude, so yes, the arts can definitely make you *feel* something! The arts also allow you to explore your creativity in many free-flowing ways. In fact, the more creative activities you participate in, the more your left and right brain communicate, and the more those hemispheres of the brain communicate, the easier it is for you to understand and regulate your emotions and actions.

Engaging in the visual arts can also improve fine motor skills. Painting and drawing require, and thus cultivate, fine motor control and hand-eye coordination. These are just a few great advantages to the visual arts—in addition to the fact that they are just plain fun!

Color-Popping Bubble Art (46)

String Art (47)

Dream Catcher (48)

Dot Art (51)

Mosaic Madness (52)

Splatter Ball Art (55)

Patchwork Collage (56)

From Markers to Paint (57)

Eye Dropper Suncatchers (58)

Sky's-the-Limit Sensory Jars (61)

Chalktopia (62)

Snow Globe (63)

Plastic Sheet Art (64)

Tissue Paper Art (65)

Name Bracelets (66)

Color-Popping Bubble Art

Kids love chasing bubbles and creating art, and this activity combines both! It will be like mystery art because they won't know where the bubbles will land or pop. Colors will also mix together, creating gorgeous new hues.

Prep: 10 minutes

Activity Time: 20 to 30 minutes

Place: Outside on a driveway or sidewalk (although this can be done inside, outside is recommended to avoid mess)

MATERIALS

Large piece of paper or roll of craft paper

3 or more mini bubble bottles with wands

Food coloring in 3 or more colors

Masking tape

STEPS

1. Place the paper outside on the pavement. Tape the corners down if desired.

2. Add a different food coloring color to each bubble bottle. Red, blue, green, and yellow work great! Add five or six drops of the color to each bottle to saturate the bubble solution. Shake it up or stir well.

3. Invite your child to blow bubbles onto the paper using the different color bubble bottles.

4. Let them blow bubbles from one color for about five minutes, then rotate to a new color. The bubbles will pop when they land on the paper, leaving rings or bubble marks. This creates a beautiful bubble artwork worthy of display!

Modification: For older children, discuss the colors that were created when the bubble prints overlapped.

Did you know? Blowing bubbles helps with visual tracking and fine motor skills. It's also a great stress reliever for children!

String Art

Ribbon and string can be made into anything! Your child can fiddle and play with the string until it is exactly where they would like it. String Art is a spin on the continuous line drawing.

Prep: 5 minutes

Activity time: 45 minutes

Place: Indoors at a solid work surface

MATERIALS

Thick white or cream-colored string

Scissors

Liquid glue, like Elmer's

Paper bowl or cup

Drawing paper

Acrylic or watercolor paint

Paint brushes

STEPS

1. Cut a piece of string between 36 and 48 inches long.

2. Pour the glue into a paper bowl or cup. Tell your child that they are going to create a work of art using this string.

3. Dip the string entirely in glue.

4. Have your child place the string onto the paper however they like. They can make shapes or pictures using the string.

5. When your child is finished with their design, allow the paper and string to dry for about 20 minutes.

6. Invite your child to paint their string art project. Make sure they sign their masterpiece!

Did you know? Painting has been proven to relieve stress and relax the body. Cool colors like blue and purple are particularly calming.

Dream Catcher

Dream catchers are a decorative item that many kids hang over their beds and associate with good dreams at night. This activity will let your child add their own flair as dream catchers can vary in color, size, shape, and texture.

Prep: 10 minutes

Activity time: 45 minutes

Environment: Indoors at a solid work surface

MATERIALS

Medium round lid, coffee can, or something circular to trace

Small poster board

Small lid, can, or something circular to trace

Scissors or box cutter

One-hole punch

Thick string or thin ribbon

Beads

Feathers

STEPS

1. Use the medium lid to trace a circle onto the poster board.

2. Inside the medium circle, use the small lid to trace a second circle in the middle of the medium circle.

3. Use scissors or a box cutter to cut the medium circle out; then cut the small circle (see Safety Tip). This will make a hoop that looks like a donut.

4. Invite your child to punch at least eight holes around the entire donut shape, closer to the inside.

5. Have your child weave the string or ribbon through the holes and across to the other side, creating a spiderweb-type pattern with the string.

6. Invite them to add beads and tie knots while they are weaving.

7. Once finished, invite your child to punch a hole and add a loop of string to the top, for hanging.

8. Punch several more holes near the bottom. They can add string, beads, and feathers to finish decorating their dream catcher.

Modification: For younger children, you can guide them in punching the holes and weaving the string. Older children may be able to use more complicated materials like wire and craft rings to create their dream catcher. They can even make it a character like a unicorn or dragon.

SAFETY TIP: Keep box cutters out of the reach of children.

Did you know? Dream catchers originated in the Ojibwa Native American culture as a way to protect children.

Dot Art

Kids love to make art, but some kids don't like to get messy. Cotton swabs make great dots and make for easy cleanup, so paint doesn't get everywhere. Let your child create patterns or objects just using dots.

Prep: 5 minutes

Activity time: 30 to 40 minutes

Place: Indoors at a solid work surface

MATERIALS

Different colored acrylic paints

Paper plate

Paper towel

Cotton swabs, like Q-Tips

Drawing paper

STEPS

1. Pour several quarter-sized puddles of different colored paints onto the paper plate. The number of colors you use is up to you.

2. On a paper towel, set out the cotton swabs (at least two per color, in case of mess-ups).

3. Invite your child to create a picture using just dots. Ask them what kind of picture they want to create. If they aren't sure, give them some choices or a starting point. Maybe a flower, an animal, or even their name in dots.

4. Encourage your child to use a new cotton swab for each color. This helps prevent colors getting muddled. Have them place the used swabs on the paper towel so they can reuse it for the same color.

Modification: For younger children, you may need to show them an example of how to use the paint and cotton swabs to create dot art.

Did you know? This is a great time to teach your child about the artist Seurat. He was best known for pointillism, the creation of art using only dots. You can find many examples online if you want to inspire your budding artist!

Mosaic Madness

This fun activity will have your child pulling things apart and piecing them back together. The combinations of shapes they'll come up with are endless. You can pick up free or cheap ceramic dishes or broken tiles at thrift stores, garage sales, or even flooring stores.

Prep: 10 minutes

Activity time: 50 minutes

Place: Indoors or outdoors

MATERIALS

Old, multicolor ceramic dishes or multicolor pieces of paper

Hammer, if using ceramics

12-by-12-inch piece of wood (for ceramic mosaic) or cardstock (for paper mosaic)

Glue suitable for the material being used, like super glue

STEPS

1. If using dishes, use a hammer to break the dishes into pieces (see Safety Tip). Cover the dishes with a towel to prevent ceramic from ricocheting.

2. Invite your child to create a picture out of small pieces and shapes. You can show them sample mosaics, if needed.

3. Encourage your child to piece things close together, explaining that it is a mosaic, not a collage. Use glue to attach the pieces.

4. Ask them which colors they like the best or what they are creating. It may be abstract so you may not be able to identify what they are making. Either way, it's okay!

SAFETY TIP: Only an adult should break the dishes, without children present. Protective eyewear should also be worn.

Did you know? Mosaics are a beautiful type of art made around the world from recycled and broken objects.

Splatter Ball Art

C'mon kids, let's get up, move, and make a mess! While super fun, this activity is also helpful for children in sports like T-ball or softball. Watch them make a home run work of art.

Prep: 10 minutes

Activity time: 30 to 45 minutes

Place: Outdoors, against fence or on a clothesline

MATERIALS

Tape or push pins

Large paper or craft roll paper

Acrylic paint in 5 colors (or water mixed with food coloring, to avoid staining the fence)

Paper plates

Disposable gloves

5 splash balls (available at most dollar stores)

STEPS

1. Tell the child they are going to create splatter art.

2. Attach the paper to the fence. Add a different colored paint to each of the paper plates.

3. Have the child put on gloves and dip a splatter ball into one color of the paint. Invite them to throw the ball at the paper anywhere they choose.

4. Next, give them the option either to dip the same color and throw it again or choose another ball dipped in another color.

5. Encourage them to continue throwing the paint-soaked balls at the paper until they are satisfied that their artwork is complete.

Modification: For older or more coordinated children, ask them if they want to be blindfolded to throw the balls or have them spin first before throwing.

Did you know? This activity helps improve hand-eye coordination while creating art.

Patchwork Collage

If your child is a fan of colorful art, set them loose on this activity. They can combine, overlap, and get as creative as they like with their patterns and shapes, without boundaries or limitations.

Prep: 5 minutes

Activity time: 30 to 60 minutes

Place: Indoors at a solid work surface

MATERIALS

Colored paper and pictures, torn or cut into various sizes and shapes

Glue

Paper to glue the pieces onto

STEPS

1. Tell your child that they are invited to create a picture out of various shapes.

2. Allow them to glue the pieces to the paper as they choose, overlapping if desired. They can create a pattern, picture, or collage.

3. Let them know the only rule is to cover all the white space. No white background should be showing when their artwork is complete.

4. If they aren't sure what to create, you can ask them guided questions: "Which of these colors do you like?" or "What kinds of things could you create with these colors?"

Did you know? Gluing small items helps children improve fine motor skills, and piecing things together to create a larger image requires and builds critical-thinking and problem-solving skills.

From Markers to Paint

Is your kid into sustainability? Good for them! This activity will let them flex their conservation muscles along with their imagination by creating new things out of old ones. Colorful things! They control how deep or vibrant the colors become. It all depends on their patience and how many old markers they've recycled. They can create a masterpiece with their newly created paint.

Prep: 5 minutes

Activity time: 1 hour

Place: Indoors at a solid work surface

MATERIALS

Recycled glass jars (such as pasta sauce jars) or Mason jars with lids

Warm water

Dried-up markers, washable

Scissors or pliers, if needed

Paper and brushes to paint with afterward

STEPS

1. Fill the jars with warm water.

2. Pull the markers apart wherever you see a seam. Use scissors or pliers to open the end of the markers if necessary (see Safety Tip).

3. Ask your child to put the ink insert in the jars with the water.

4. Allow the ink to sit for as long as needed to get the desired saturation of color. The more ink you use, the deeper the color saturation will be.

5. Invite your child to use the watercolors they created to make a painting. Have them come up with their own idea of what they would like to paint.

6. Store the leftover watercolors in sealed containers for future use. They can be used for painting or coloring homemade play dough, too!

SAFETY TIP: Scissors may be required to cut open the markers. An adult should do this part, or if the child is older, supervise and assist as needed.

Did you know? Crayola offers a free marker recycling program to schools. Learn more at crayola.com/colorcycle.

Eye Dropper Suncatchers

This activity is so much fun, especially for children who like to create abstract art. It's also fun for children who like structure in their art as they can cut it into any shape afterward. It's the best of both worlds, and a different way to engage in art.

Prep: 5 minutes

Activity time: 30 minutes

Place: Indoors at a solid work surface, or outdoors on a driveway or sidewalk (for a cleaner option)

MATERIALS

Newspaper to protect the work surface (if indoors)

Coffee filters

Eye or medicine dropper

Food coloring or homemade watercolors, see From Markers to Paint (page 57)

String or ribbon

STEPS

1. Lay down newspaper if indoors. Place the coffee filter on the newspaper or pavement (if outdoors).

2. Show your child how to use the dropper to soak up liquid. Explain to them how less is better—if the coffee filter is too soaked, it will take a long time to dry.

3. Allow them to use different colors and create any pattern they want. It will look almost like tie-dye with the edges of the colors blending together.

4. Allow their art to dry, attach string, and hang it in a window. Voilà!

Did you know? It may just look like fun, but this activity cultivates many skills, including fine motor, creative thinking, and color effects (how red and yellow come together to make orange), to name a few!

Sky's-the-Limit Sensory Jars

Children of all ages will get immersed in this project—I've even made a few for myself. Offer your child all sorts of tiny objects to customize their sensory jars; they can add anything of interest into the bottle. Each one is unique and mesmerizing to view.

Prep: 5 minutes

Activity time: 20 to 30 minutes

Place: Indoors or outdoors at a solid work surface

MATERIALS

Plastic bottle with cap (like a water or sports drink bottle)

Small funnel

Water or oil or both

Glitter

Small objects, like sequins or beads

Food coloring or glow-in-the-dark paint (optional)

Hot glue gun

STEPS

1. Remove any labels from the bottle.

2. Open the bottle. Using a funnel, invite your child to add water and/or oil until the bottle is about 80 percent full.

3. Using the dried funnel or fingers, invite your child to add glitter—the chunkier the pieces, the better.

4. Have your child add any other desired items until they have added everything that they want.

5. Have your child add a few drops of food coloring or glow-in-the-dark paint so it will glow with the lights out.

6. Add hot glue to the inside rim of the cap, then screw the cap on to close the bottle permanently (see Safety Tip).

SAFETY TIP: An adult should operate the hot glue gun. Keep the hot glue gun out of your child's reach.

Did you know? In addition to the creative joy of making them, sensory bottles are a great refocusing and calming tool.

Chalktopia

Let your child get their mural-designing jam on! This fun activity combines outside time, sunshine, and imagination! You may want to lead into this activity by showing your child some examples of murals created by other artists.

Prep: None

Activity time: 20 to 30 minutes

Place: Outdoors on a driveway or sidewalk

MATERIALS

Multicolored chalk

STEPS

1. Give your child the container of chalk.

2. Tell them that they have been commissioned to create a mural on the sidewalk. If they don't know, you can explain that a mural is a large-scale piece of art.

3. Set them loose to create anything they'd like! Ask questions about their mural as they design it.

Modification: If your child needs guidance, ask them what kinds of places they like to go. Older children may prefer liquid chalk spray, which can create more of a graffiti-type artwork on the sidewalk.

Tip: Take a picture, because the rain will wash their beautiful art away. If they want to start over, just clean it with a hose and start again fresh the next day!

Snow Globe

I don't know if snow globes ever lose their magical appeal; they seem to bring out the child in everyone! Let your child create their own mesmerizing snow globe. Snow globes don't have to be holiday-themed—let your child customize theirs. Maybe they want to make a unicorn snow globe and use rainbow glitter. Whatever's magic to them is the best theme!

Prep: 5 minutes

Activity time: 30 minutes

Place: Indoors at a solid work surface near an electrical outlet

MATERIALS

Hot glue gun

Figurine small enough to fit in the jar

Baby food jar, cleaned and label removed

Glitter (white, colored, or transparent)

Water

STEPS

1. Plug in the hot glue gun (see Safety Tip).

2. Let the child choose a figurine to glue onto the inside of the lid. Using the hot glue gun, glue it on for them.

3. Let them add a pinch of glitter or confetti to the jar.

4. Let them add enough water to the jar to nearly fill it.

5. Add hot glue to the inside rim of the lid, then attach it to the jar.

6. Invite them to shake and enjoy their snow globe!

SAFETY TIP: An adult should operate the hot glue gun. Keep the hot glue gun out of your child's reach.

Tip: You can make your own snow globe while they are making one. You may pick up great ideas from each other!

Did you know? This snow globe can be used as a calming/soothing tool for kids.

Plastic Sheet Art

This activity puts a creative spin on your typical watercolor painting activity. By painting on plastic, followed by wetting and smearing onto paper, you'll create new designs and color combinations.

Prep: 5 minutes

Activity time: 20 minutes

Place: Indoors or outdoors at a solid work surface

MATERIALS

Scissors

Plastic page protector sheet

Watercolor paper (You can use regular paper, but it may crinkle with the water)

Washable markers

Spray bottle with water

STEPS

1. Cut the sheet protector along the bottom so it opens like a book. Place the paper on the right side of the open plastic protector.

2. Invite your child to draw any design on the left side of the plastic (across from the paper) with at least three different colors.

3. Have them spray the design just once with the spray bottle (enough to wet but not soak).

4. Have them close the plastic over the paper.

5. Have your child slide their hand across the plastic sheet. This will create a watercolor effect on the paper.

6. Lift the plastic and reveal the design. Now they have a beautiful watercolor background. They can create any art they want on top of it or leave it as-is.

Modification: Invite older children to print a saying or quote on the watercolor paper when it's dry. They can even frame it in an inexpensive frame.

Tissue Paper Art

Tissue paper isn't just for wrapping gifts. In this activity, it is used to create the gift of original and oh-so-colorful artwork!

Prep: None

Activity time: 30 to 45 minutes

Place: Indoors at a solid work surface

MATERIALS

Tissue paper, various colors

Glue

Wide paint brush

Drawing paper

STEPS

1. Tell your child they are going to create art out of tissue paper and have them rip the tissue paper into small pieces any way they choose.

2. Next, have them brush glue onto the paper and attach the tissue paper however they like.

3. If you would like to guide them, you can ask: "What would you like to create with the tissue?" or "What shapes would you need?"

Did you know? Even just tearing paper helps improve fine motor skills. It also has been proven to be a great way to calm emotions.

Name Bracelets

Jewelry-making and fine motor skills come together in this fun personalization project. Kids love things with their name on them, so they may want to make these bracelets for all their friends, too!

Prep: 5 minutes

Activity time: 15 to 30 minutes

Place: Anywhere at a solid work surface

MATERIALS

Pipe cleaners (for younger kids). Use one pipe cleaner for smaller wrists, and two pipe cleaners for larger wrists.

8-inch pieces of string (for older kids)

Colored beads

Alphabet beads

Tape

STEPS

1. If using a pipe cleaner, loop one end to prevent beads from falling off. If using string, tape one end to the table.

2. Have your child choose six to eight colored beads and place them on the pipe cleaner or string.

3. Have the child place each letter of their name on the pipe cleaner or string.

4. Have them place six to eight more colored beads on the pipe cleaner or string.

5. Fit the bracelet to their wrist, adding more beads, if needed. If using pipe cleaners, twist the ends to meet, smoothing out any sharp points. If using string, simply tie the two ends together.

Did you know? Letter beads are a creative way to practice names, sight words, and vocabulary words.

MUSIC

Have you ever listened to a song and gotten chills? Or, were you suddenly transported to a specific place, time, or person? Music can generate powerful feelings inside us, and this isn't without positive consequence. Music can have tremendous effects on child development and has been researched for its benefits in all kinds of situations and therapies. Music helps release emotions in a positive way—it helps calm, soothe, motivate, and uplift. Engaging in music affects both the left side of the brain, normally associated with academic reasoning or logic, and the right side, known as the creative hemisphere of the brain. Both hemispheres work together when creating or listening to music, and this can create new pathways or connections in the brain.

Make and Shake

This activity combines the creative pursuits of art and music. Let your child choose from a variety of items to fill their instrument; each creation will make different noises on the inside.

Prep: None

Activity time: 15 to 20 minutes

Place: Indoors at a solid work surface for the construction part. Anywhere for the dancing part.

MATERIALS

1 or more paper plates (1 per music shaker)

Dry beans, buttons, or pennies

Stapler

Markers

STEPS

1. Set out the paper plate.

2. Have your child place the beans or pennies on the plate, then carefully fold the plate in half.

3. Use a stapler to staple the rim of the paper plate together so that the contents don't fall out. The shape should be a semicircle once stapled.

4. Invite your child to color the shaker with markers in any design they'd like.

5. Create music with the child—sing, dance, and have them shake their shaker to the beat.

Modification: For older children, you can play different types of music and see if they can follow along with the beat.

Did you know? Music has proven effective for helping children de-stress and relax.

Rhythm and Emotions Musical Painting

This 2-in-1 activity lets children get in touch with their emotions as they learn to identify the music and colors that give them the good feels!

Prep: 5 minutes

Activity Time: 15 to 20 minutes

Place: Indoors or outdoors at a solid surface or easel

MATERIALS

Music (see Tip)

Paper

Watercolors or washable paint

Paint brushes

STEPS

EMOTIONS OPTION

1. Tell your child they are going to paint how the music makes them feel.

2. Turn on some music and ask your child how the music makes them feel.

3. Tell them to paint how the music makes them feel.

4. Now, change to a different type of music, and ask them to paint how it makes them feel. They can describe their emotions while painting.

5. Repeat with as many types of music as you want (country, pop, classical, etc.). You can have them compare their feelings between the different types of music.

RHYTHM OPTION

1. Tell your child they are going to paint to the tempo or beat of the music.

2. Turn on music and have your child paint to the tempo of the music.

3. Change the type of music and have them paint to the tempo of a different style.

4. Have a conversation with them about which tempo they liked best and why.

5. Encourage them to sing as they paint!

Tip: You can download iHeartRadio for free (iheart .com)! If any of the watercolor or washable paints get on your child's clothes, use a little dish soap to get it out of the fabric easier.

Did you know? Music has been proven to increase brain function, enhance memory, and help develop better language skills.

DIY Rain Stick

Rain sticks are traditionally made from dried-out cacti, but we won't do that. Instead, your child will repurpose cardboard tubes for this fun activity. Perfect for children who like to make noise and are constantly tapping on tables, chairs, doors, or themselves, this activity integrates a little crafting, artwork, music, and dance moves. They can use this rain stick for fun, but as a bonus, the soothing sounds will calm their minds.

Prep: 5 minutes

Activity time: 30 to 40 minutes

Place: Indoors or outdoors

MATERIALS

2 (5-by-5-inch) squares of plastic wrap

Paper towel or wrapping paper tube

2 rubber bands

$\frac{1}{4}$ to $\frac{3}{4}$ cup pea-sized dried beans

Washable markers

STEPS

1. Attach one of the plastic wrap squares to an end of the paper towel tube with a rubber band. Press on the plastic wrap to make sure it's secure.

2. Have your child pour some beans inside the tube.

3. Attach the remaining plastic wrap square to the other end of the paper towel tube with the rubber band.

4. Invite your child to decorate their rain stick with the markers.

5. Now, tell your child to tip the stick back and forth to get the rain sound.

6. Invite your child to create a dance to go with their new rain stick!

Modification: If you need to guide a younger child, ask what ways they can move their rain stick and how the sound makes them feel. Then, let them dance how they feel.

Tip: You can use Mod Podge, or other sealer, as a clear coat over your decorated rain stick to keep the art from smudging.

Did you know? Rain sticks can be used to increase cognitive ability by demonstrating cause and effect when turned from side to side.

Cup Tap Challenge

Is your child a musical kid who likes to tap on things, make sounds, and move to their own beat? Here is a super cool activity that puts them in charge of coming up with a rhythm that turns into a song. Show them "cup tapping" on YouTube to give them an idea of this rhythmic style.

Prep: None

Activity time: 15 to 20 minutes

Place: Indoors or outdoors on a hard surface like a floor or table

MATERIALS

Plastic cups

Music (optional)

STEPS

1. Invite your child to tap the cups on the ground or other surfaces to make a beat and create a song.

2. You can play music so they can get a beat to use as an example while they create their own.

3. Invite your child to use different types of cups to create different sounds!

Modification: Older or more musically inclined children can create lyrics to go with their cup rhythm.

Did you know? Activities like cup tapping help increase hand-eye coordination, gross motor skills, and rhythm.

Rhythm of Nature

Think about all the noises you hear in the world around you. Loud sounds, soft sounds and in-between... When these beats combine, they create an organic rhythm pattern. Nature has its own unique melody. The wind going whoosh. The whistle of an approaching storm. What about the babble of a stream of water? Or the sound of a dog's feet on the sidewalk? What outside sounds can you replicate using only the parts of your body? Listen carefully and make your own personal beat.

Prep: None

Activity time: 20 minutes

Place: Outdoors

MATERIALS

Pencil

Paper

Stopwatch, timer, or clock (optional)

STEPS

1. Tell your child to sit for 5 minutes and think of the different sounds from nature around them.

2. Next, have them choose one of the sounds and pick a body part: mouth, arm, leg, foot, etc. Instruct them to imitate the sound with their body part of choice 2 or more times.

3. Have them write or draw this sound on paper and how many times they have used it. You will repeat this step by choosing 4 additional sounds to record on paper.

4. Invite them to perform their completed beat combination for you or someone else. The paper will be their sheet music, so they can play their personal beat anytime.

Bell Bracelet Tambourines

This activity works on fine motor skills as your child gets to make up their own rhythm and dance moves while having some musical fun. They can get as inventive as they wish.

Prep: 10 minutes

Activity time: 20 to 30 minutes

Place: Indoors at a solid work surface to make the bell tambourines, and anywhere for the dancing

MATERIALS

Jingle bells

Jewelry wire, medium strength, cut to fit the child's wrist (see Safety Tip), or pipe cleaners

Wire cutter or scissors, if needed

STEPS

1. Invite your child to take as many bells as they would like and attach them to the wire or pipe cleaner.

2. Once completed, twist the wire ends or pipe cleaners together.

3. Invite your child to wear their bracelet tambourines and use them to create music to the beat of the jingle. They can even sing along.

Modification: Older kids can create jingle tambourines for their ankles, too. They make it more challenging to keep a beat.

SAFETY TIP: An adult should cut the jewelry wire with wire cutters or scissors.

Drum It Up

Start off by giving your child artistic freedom to design their drum patterns and colors, then set them off to tap and make noise to their heart's content, with or without musical accompaniment!

Prep: 5 minutes

Activity time: 20 to 40 minutes

Place: Indoors or outdoors at a solid work surface

MATERIALS

2 (9-by-9-inch) sheets wax paper

Large coffee can or other large tin can (see Tip)

2 large rubber bands

Paint

Paint brushes

STEPS

1. Place the wax paper over the open end of the can, and attach it with a large rubber band.

2. Cover the wax paper with a second layer of wax paper secured with another rubber band for added strength.

3. Invite your child to paint or decorate the sides of the drum however they would like and allow it to dry.

4. Once the paint has dried, let your child drum away, creating any rhythm they want.

5. Repeat these directions to make other sized drums if your musician wants more than one!

Modification: For older children, see if they can play multiple drums at once while keeping a rhythm.

Tip: Tin/metal cans make the best reverberating drum sound.

Sustainable Guitar

Your child can make their own guitar from recycled items. Let them try this and the drum (page 77) and see which they prefer—they may love both!

Prep: 5 minutes

Activity time: 40 to 50 minutes

Place: Indoors or outdoors at a solid work surface

MATERIALS

Paint and brushes (optional)

Shoe box or rectangular tissue box with hole in top

Hot glue gun

Paint stir stick

Variety of stretchy rubber bands or nylon string

Stapler

STEPS

1. Invite your child to paint the outside of the box if desired, and then allow it to dry.

2. Hot glue the paint stir stick vertically on the back side of the box (see Safety Tip).

3. Have your child attach rubber bands around the box widthwise. The rubber bands need to be large enough to go around the entire box without collapsing it (see Tip).

4. If you are using nylon strings instead, you can staple them end to end across the front of the box over the hole.

5. Invite your child to use their guitar to create beautiful music!

SAFETY TIP: An adult should operate the hot glue gun. Keep the hot glue gun out of your child's reach.

Tip: The tighter the rubber bands or strings, the higher the note they will produce. Use various degrees of tightness to create different sounds.

Did you know? Learning to create a rhythm can improve concentration. It can also increase muscle memory and processing skills.

Emoji Tunes

Music brings out the creativity in all of us, and whether your child has a flair for the dramatic or keeps their feelings inside, this activity will put them "in tune" with their feelings. Let your child discover the feelings and thoughts that different kinds of music bring to the surface. Parents, you may be surprised by what you'll learn about your child and their complex feelings, too.

Prep: 10 minutes

Activity time: 20 to 30 minutes

Place: Indoors or outdoors near a music source

MATERIALS

Music, various types

STEPS

1. Tell your child they are going to dance the way that the music makes them feel.

2. Play some music. If they're stuck, you can ask them, "Does this make you feel happy or sad?" "How do you dance when you are happy?" and "What would sad dancing look like?"

3. Invite them to dance to different types of music.

4. They can describe their emotions with words and dance or just through dance.

Modification: If your child seems ready, you can ask them why a certain piece of music made them feel a certain way. Did it remind them of something or someone? Listen to their thoughts and support their expressed feelings.

Did you know? It takes deep critical-thinking skills and an innate awareness of their emotions for children to transform how they are feeling into dance.

Beatbox Bonanza

Does your child know about beatboxing? Find "beatboxing" and "body percussion" on YouTube to inspire them, and then let them make musical patterns with sounds from their body and mouth to create their own songs.

Prep: None

Activity time: 30 minutes

Place: Anywhere

MATERIALS

Paper and markers (optional)

STEPS

1. Explain to your child they can come up with a series of snaps, claps, and stomps to make a creative patterned song. Watch some YouTubers together to learn about different sounds they can make.

2. If they would like to keep track of their tune, they can record it on paper using symbols for the sounds; for example, smiley face means snap, square means clap, oval means stomp.

3. Invite them to perform their pattern song for you or anyone they'd like!

Did you know? Remembering and performing patterns in movements requires and builds brain power and coordination.

Hooping to the Tune

If your kid has extra energy they need to get out, bring on the Hula-Hoops! Hula-hooping is a great way to release that energy, and adding music makes it even more fun! It also adds a bit of challenge when trying to hoop to the tempo of the music.

Prep: None

Activity time: 20 minutes

Place: Indoors in an open area or outdoors

MATERIALS

1 or more Hula-Hoops

Music

STEPS

1. Invite your child to dance to different music with the Hula-Hoop.

2. Encourage them to increase or decrease their speed based on the tempo of the music.

3. Tell your child that the Hula-Hoop can be used in creative ways, not just on their hips. Use arms, legs, or necks, too.

Modification: Older or more coordinated children can add to the challenge by using multiple hoops at once—just make sure they have enough space not to knock into things!

Did you know? A woman once hooped for 72 hours in 1984. And somebody set a record by hooping with 105 hoops at one time in 2007. That takes some creative moves—and practice!

Rhyme in Time

The child who is always singing or making up songs will love creating their own music with this activity. Rhyming words and creating lyrics adds to the challenge. Bring this activity on your next road trip to pass the miles!

Prep: None

Activity time: 15 minutes

Place: Anywhere

MATERIALS

Instrumental music (without lyrics)

STEPS

1. Allow your child to come up with some rhyming pairs, or you can give them samples.

2. Once they choose a pair, invite your child to make a two-sentence lyric to the beat of the music. For example, if they chose rhyming words "go" and "snow," their lyrics might be "There is a place I'd like to go. It's blue and warm and has no snow."

3. Have your child choose another rhyming pair and continue with a different type of music.

Modification: If your child is a natural at this game, take turns and come up with rhyming lyrics on cue with the music. It will require quick thinking and may result in some hilarious nonsense lyrics!

Did you know? Thinking on their feet like this helps children with improvisational life skills. They learn how to think deeply and critically.

Create-a-Xylophone

If your child enjoyed making a drum (page 77) and a guitar (page 79), it may be time to take things to the next level with the xylophone! This activity will let your child be a miniature carpenter by building a large-scale instrument. They can add their artistic touch by decorating their instrument and bring it to life by making beautiful music!

Prep: 15 to 20 minutes

Activity time: 30 to 40 minutes

Place: Indoors or outdoors

MATERIALS

2 pieces of 1 inch x 2 inch x 1 foot furring strips (see Tip).

Wood glue

6 to 8 (21-inch) paint stir sticks, cut crosswise into different lengths (start with a 4-inch length, then cut each one 1 to 2 inches longer than the last, depending on how many "keys" you want)

Acrylic paints

Paint brushes

2 small (6-inch long) dowels or 2 metal spoons

STEPS

1. Lay the furring strip pieces at a 45-degree angle, but do not allow the ends to meet or overlap where the angle narrows. (Be sure to allow 2 inches of space between the two furring strip pieces at the bottom.)

2. Next, glue the 3-inch paint stir stick piece on top of the two strips about 1-inch from the bottom. Leave 2 inches in between each staggered piece of wood and repeat with the next size up.

3. Continue this process, from smallest to largest, until all the pieces are attached between the two strips.

4. Allow the instrument to dry, and then invite your child to paint it as they would like.

5. Once dry, offer your child the two dowel sticks or metal spoons to create some music on their new xylophone!

Tip: If you buy the wood at a home improvement store, most will cut the pieces for free.

Egg Shaker Fun

Plastic eggs make awesome instruments. Your child will enjoy choosing their colors and choosing the items they put inside. Encourage them to make a whole variety of musical egg shakers so they can make different sounds and beats to the music.

Prep: None

Activity time: 15 to 20 minutes

Place: Anywhere

MATERIALS

Plastic eggs

Pennies, beans, bells—anything that will jingle

Scotch tape

Popsicle sticks or plastic spoons

STEPS

1. Invite your child to choose a plastic egg and open it up.

2. Let them fill the egg halfway with pennies or other jingling items. Encourage them not to overfill the egg so the items can move around.

3. Have your child close the eggs and tape the seam if desired.

4. If your child would like the shakers to have handles, they can tape a Popsicle stick on each side or tape a plastic spoon to both sides. Either will make the egg sturdier.

5. Use the egg shakers to create music.

Did you know? It may seem simple, but allowing a child to choose what they put inside the egg gives them confidence in making more creative choices.

Musical Scavenger Hunt

Let's go on a hunt for sounds! This activity has a puzzle-solving component that will require their ears and brain to work together. It's a creative twist on a scavenger hunt, with a jam session at the end!

Prep: 10 to 15 minutes

Activity time: 30 to 45 minutes

Place: Indoors or outdoors

MATERIALS

Recorded sounds from household objects (Examples: two forks clanging together, a wooden spoon and metal pot, alarm clock, timer, zipper, door squeaking or shutting, etc.)

STEPS

1. Tell your child they are going on a sound hunt.

2. Play the recording and allow them to hear a sound. Repeat the sound multiple times or allow them to play it multiple times.

3. Set them off hunting for the objects and see if they can find the item that replicates the sound.

4. Once all items are collected, see if they'd like to use the objects to create a song.

DANCE AND MOVEMENT

The waltz, the twist, air guitar, the floss—dance is truly timeless, and why not? Kids need to move! Dance is, of course, just one form of movement—whether you do an exercise routine, wave a flag and march, or practice animal moves, it all counts as creative fun. Both dance and movement are also critical to brain development. Research has shown that dance and movement positively affect the hippocampus region of the brain, responsible for long- and short-term memory and even balance! Plus, dance and movement are proven to be even more effective than regular exercise as they require more memory and brain function than simple exercises. Getting moving at a young age also promotes a healthy lifestyle, so get your child dancing for long-lasting, positive effects on their body and mind.

Scarf Dancing (88)

Interpretive Storytelling (90)

Balancing Act (91)

Tightrope Challenge (92)

A-maze-ing Race (93)

Obstacle Build-and-Go (94)

Animal Acting (96)

Dicey Moves (97)

A Pirate's Life for Me! (98)

A Hop, a Gallop, and a Slither (99)

Scarf Dancing

What is it about a scarf that brings out the dancer in a child? Silky scarves are graceful and flowy and allow the child to move in any way they feel. To their scarf dance, they can add leaps, jumps, twirls—the works. Dancing with a prop like this can be loads of fun.

Prep: None

Activity time: 15 to 20 minutes

Place: Anywhere

MATERIALS

Long silky scarf (the lighter, the better)

Music (optional)

STEPS

1. Give your child a scarf and invite them to create a dance with it.

2. You can guide them by giving suggestions like zig-zagging or leaping with the scarf.

3. Add music if it gives them inspiration.

4. Offer descriptive praise as they make choices for dancing.

Interpretive Storytelling

Make your child the storyteller—without speaking any words. In this activity, your child will use dramatic movement to tell a story with their body. It's a great form of exercise and takes some creative thinking to form movements that tell a story.

Prep: None

Activity time: 15 to 20 minutes

Place: Anywhere

MATERIALS

Background music (optional)

STEPS

1. Ask your child to choose a topic they like; for example, unicorns or a sunset.

2. Invite them to create a series of movements to tell a story about the topic they chose. They can add music if they want to, but their movements should tell the story.

3. Afterward, encourage them to describe the story they were telling and why they chose the movements they did to represent their story.

4. Let them repeat with as many topics as they would like.

Balancing Act

Yoga is not only good for stretching your body, it's also good for your mind, whether you're a child or an adult. It is also very useful for helping relieve stress. This activity will allow children to work on balance and muscle memory while moving in some flexible, creative ways.

Prep: None, unless it needs to be guided (see Modification)

Activity time: 15 to 20 minutes

Place: Indoors or outdoors on the ground

MATERIALS

Yoga mat, or carpeted or grassy space

STEPS

1. Tell your child that they are going to exercise their mind and body with some stretches.

2. Show them the poses, one at a time, and tell them the name of the pose. Let them assume each position for 10 to 20 seconds.

3. Offer modifications if balance isn't their strength, but remember, balance will improve the more they practice yoga.

Modification: If a child needs guidance or doesn't have great balance, you can offer yoga pose cards to give them ideas. Free printouts are available online at sites like Pinterest.

Tightrope Challenge

Did you ever notice that kids like to balance and walk on curbs like they are on a high wire? Here's an activity that offers them the chance to pretend they are a tightrope walker without leaving the ground!

Prep: 5 to 10 minutes

Activity time: 20 to 30 minutes

Place: indoors or outdoors on solid ground

MATERIALS

4 or 5 jump ropes

Tape or weights

STEPS

1. Tape the jump ropes to the ground in a variety of ways, such as straight lines, zigzags, swirls, and twists and turns. Leave one rope free.

2. Explain that you have made a tightrope course for your child and that they are going to try balancing on the jump ropes without falling off.

3. Have them complete the course. If they fall off, then they must start over.

4. Invite them to use the last jump rope to create a challenge of their own.

Modification: Older or more coordinated children can hop on one foot for the entire course, to make it more challenging.

A-maze-ing Race

Your child is stuck in the maze; how will they get out before sundown? They'll get to navigate through the maze and redirect navigation when they reach a wrong turn. Once they see how it works, they can create their own maze for you or their friends.

Prep: 5 to 10 minutes

Activity time: 10 to 15 minutes

Place: Outdoors on a large, hard area such as a driveway

MATERIALS

Chalk

STEPS

1. Using chalk, create a maze on the sidewalk or driveway.

2. Tell your child that it's their job to navigate through this maze. Explain that there are dead ends, so watch out.

3. Have them create their own maze to share with friends.

Modification: For older children who enjoy a challenge, tell them if they reach a dead end, they must start over.

Did you know? Puzzles are a good workout for the brain and help strengthen memory skills.

Obstacle Build-and-Go

Obstacle courses are excellent rainy day activities and can be made from anything, like piles of books to crab-walk over. They give children an opportunity to jump, run, play, and have tons of fun while moving. Children can help create the obstacle course, which makes it more hands-on, exciting, and, yes, creative for them.

Prep: 10 minutes

Activity time: 20 to 30 minutes

Place: Indoors or outdoors in an open area

MATERIALS

Items for creating an obstacle course (such as boxes, cones, jump ropes, Hula-Hoops, pillows, cushions, chairs, balls, etc.)

Timer (optional)

STEPS

1. Set up an obstacle course in whatever way you want. For example, you might place Hula-Hoops on the ground to hop through, followed by a jump rope tightrope, then safety cones that they can weave through with a ball between their legs, followed by an open box to crawl through. Try to add variety, such as high and low obstacles.

2. Ready, set, go! Present the obstacle course to your child. If desired, tell them to show how fast they can complete it, and time them.

3. Once the obstacle course is completed, they can do it again if they want to beat their time or just have fun.

4. When they've mastered the course, invite them to try different ways to complete it, such as on one foot or blindfolded. If blindfolded, make sure there are no sharp edges, hazards, or jumping challenges required.

5. Invite your child to use these same items to create their own obstacle course, and then complete it. Invite some friends to try it out!

Animal Acting

Does your child have extra energy? In this activity, they'll get to act like animals and move like them, too. They can get as detailed and extravagant with their moves as they want.

Prep: None

Activity time: 15 to 20 minutes

Place: Anywhere

MATERIALS

Picture cards featuring animals

STEPS

1. Without looking, have your child pull an animal card. That is their animal. Have them move as if they were transformed into that animal.

2. Allow them to continue pulling cards and acting out their animal movements. They can also incorporate other animals of their choice or tell a story along with their animal movements.

Modification: Older children may enjoy pulling two cards, then creating how that morphed animal would move.

Dicey Moves

Shake, roll, and move to a variety of positions that your child chooses. What will the move be this time? Roll the dice and see!

Prep: 5 to 10 minutes

Activity time: 20 to 30 minutes

Place: Anywhere

MATERIALS

1 number die

1 write-and-wipe die

Music (optional)

STEPS

1. Let your child draw or write a different movement on each side of a write-and-wipe die or square box. Explain to the child that they are going to roll the die, and then do the actions it asks them to do. For example, if the number die says three and the write-and-wipe die says jump, they will do three jumps.

2. You can also raise the movement requirements by adding more number dice.

3. You can turn on music if you'd like, so they can do the movements to a beat.

Modification: To make it more challenging, roll three sets of dice with movements and numbers; they must complete them all back-to-back. See if your child can remember the order.

Did you know? Movement is great for brain development and overall health. Thirty minutes of active movement a day makes a big difference.

A Pirate's Life for Me!

Who doesn't like to dress up and be someone else? In this activity, children get to pretend to be a pirate—voice, movements, and all. But be careful. Their new pirate persona may make you walk the plank!

Prep: 5 minutes

Activity time: 10 to 20 minutes

Place: Anywhere

MATERIALS

Materials to create a pirate outfit and pirate props (such as a hat, eye patch, ragged clothing, child's sword, big box for a ship, paper for the plank, play jewelry or coins for treasure)

STEPS

1. Gather materials to create a pirate outfit and pirate props.

2. Announce: "Ahoy there, matey! Today you're a pirate. You're going to move like a pirate through the house searching for treasure—and someone may walk the plank!"

3. Set your child on their pirate adventure and be a good audience for them, listening to their story as they go. Let them show you the loot they were able to find.

Modification: You can add challenges along the way. For example, pretend this pirate has a balance problem. Tell them they may have to get creative as they move about.

A Hop, a Gallop, and a Slither

How does a snake slither? How does an animal with four legs gallop? And how does a kangaroo jump so far in one leap? Let your child imagine what it's like to move like an animal.

Prep: 10 minutes

Activity time: 20 to 30 minutes

Place: Indoors or outdoors

MATERIALS

20 cards with either hop, gallop, or slither written on them (add pictures if needed)

4 index cards

STEPS

1. Have them put a movement of their choice on the 4 blank cards.

2. Let your child, without looking, choose a card and do that movement.

3. Next, choose another card and do the same until all the cards are used. Ask your child what kind of animals make the movement they're doing. If they hop, for example, are they doing a little bird hop or a racing hare hop? Let them show you the difference.

Modification: To make it more challenging, you can add numbers to the cards; for instance, 2 hops, 3 slithers, etc. You can also give a sequence of directions and let your child see if they can remember all the movements in the right order.

Chapter Four

Let's Create: Role Play!

This chapter is all about the drama; that is, role playing and learning to improvise or think on the spot. Improvisation and dramatic play-type activities allow children to experience situations using their imagination. Even though they're fun, these activities require critical-thinking skills and help brain development. These types of activities can also aid children in becoming more flexible by enabling them to improvise when things don't go their way. An easy way to draw children into these types of activities is to center them around their favorite things to watch or play with, or any subject they are interested in. Do they like sports? Baking? Dolls? Anime? Traveling? Whatever it is, you can role play with that.

Prop Charades

This game is a spin on traditional charades, adding the element of props. Your child will get an opportunity to use objects in a multitude of ways to help them convey what they are acting—of course, without words. It takes a lot of imagination and brain power to use objects in a way they are not intended to be used!

Prep: 10 minutes

Activity time: 30 minutes

Place: Indoors or outdoors

MATERIALS

Props (hats, spoons, pans, socks, etc.) in a container

Cards with actions or items to act out (surprised, baseball, queen, elephant, etc.)

2 or more people

Stopwatch or clock (optional)

STEPS

1. Explain to your child that they are going to pull a card and act out the item on it without using words. They can use gestures and any of the props in the container.

2. The teammate has to guess what the child is acting out.

3. Continue until time is up.

4. Take turns and keep track of points, which are scored when a teammate guesses the intended action before time runs out. Play to 5 or 10, or just play for fun and don't keep score at all.

Modification: For children who don't read yet, include pictures on the card with the word so they know what to act out.

Don't Fall In!

This activity is right up there with homemade tents as a fun and creative activity for a rainy day. Don't Fall In! is going to take imagination, some fancy maneuvering, and a bit of creativity to avoid falling in the hot lava.

Prep: 10 minutes

Activity time: 20 minutes

Place: An indoor area with floor space

MATERIALS

4 to 6 pillows or cushions

4 chairs (or other items kids can safely climb on)

STEPS

1. Set up chairs and pillows all around the floor. Starting at a certain part of the room, tell your child they can't touch the floor because it's covered in lava.

2. They can move pillows or chairs as needed to get from one side of the room to the other, but they cannot touch the floor—or else!

Modification: To make it more challenging, limit the number of pillows to two and the chairs to one. You can also spread the pillows and chairs farther apart, requiring the child to get much more flexible and inventive with their movements.

Did you know? More than just fun, this activity helps practice and strengthen gross motor skills and balance.

Mirror, Mirror

A simple mirror can create so much fun! This activity lets kids imitate others and make up random movements with their face, hands, and body.

Prep: None

Activity time: 15 minutes

Place: Indoors or outdoors

MATERIALS

2 people or more (if more, you can pair them up)

Large mirror

STEPS

1. Child 1 performs an action facing the mirror.

2. Child 2 does their best to mirror the first child's action.

3. Both do the action at the same time facing the mirror.

4. Child 2 chooses the next action.

5. Child 1 repeats the action.

6. Both do the action at the same time.

7. Try to make the action more complicated or creative each time. Add music if you like so making faces in time to the beat becomes the challenge.

8. Continue until you have done at least 10 mirroring actions.

Modification: Children who know sign language can add signing words or phrases in between their mirror moves to make it more challenging.

Zombie for a Day

Kids are obsessed with zombies. This activity gets the imagination going by allowing them to take on the dramatic role of a zombie. A zombie is so different from us that it will take some creative thinking to achieve. Why stop at zombies? Kids can be dragons, unicorns, Transformers, or anything else they can dream up!

Prep: None

Activity time: 15 minutes

Place: Anywhere

MATERIALS

Picture/word cards, if needed for guidance on how to act like a zombie, or with additional ideas (unicorns, dragons, etc.)

STEPS

1. Tell your child that they are going to act like a zombie for a day.

2. Give them a few minutes to think about what it would be like.

3. Let them tell a story about their day in the life of a zombie (in a zombie voice, of course) and act out their story.

4. Invite them to choose another character to become if they wish.

Modification: Step up the challenge by inviting them to switch back and forth between two characters, such as a zombie and a unicorn. When you say "switch," they must switch to the other character. Older kids can also write a script to go with their zombie experience.

What's My Character?

Timeless storybook characters come to life in this activity that allows children to jump into starring roles. Can you guess who they are? Can they guess who you are? We'll see!

Prep: 15 minutes

Activity time: 30 minutes

Place: Anywhere

MATERIALS

Index cards or small pieces of paper

2 or more people

STEPS

1. On index cards or paper, write the name of a favorite story character, one on each card. For younger children, draw or cut out a picture of the character.

2. Tell your child you are going to act out a character from a favorite story.

3. Choose a card. Act like a character from that story.

4. Let the child(ren) try to guess the character you are representing.

5. If someone guesses it correctly, it's their turn to act. Make sure everyone gets a turn to act.

Modification: Older children can choose a card and reenact the whole story as the cast of characters.

Go With the Motion

Kids will love exploring the infinite number of ways they can move their bodies. In this activity, children will test their memory as they creatively evolve one movement into another.

Prep: None

Activity time: 10 minutes

Place: Anywhere

MATERIALS

4 or more people

STEPS

1. The first person does any kind of movement.

2. The second person takes that movement, repeats it, and then turns it into a slightly different movement.

3. This continues child to child until the 10 minutes are up.

4. At the end, see if the children can remember and perform the first and last move to see how it evolved.

Modification: Challenge older kids to do multiple consecutive moves that the next person needs to extend and change.

Did you know? Creative movement is great for muscle memory.

First and Last

First and Last is a great collaborative activity for children. Here they'll get to bounce ideas off other people and use their imagination freely to create and act out their own sensational story.

Prep: 10 minutes

Activity time: 10 to 20 minutes

Place: Anywhere

MATERIALS

Cards with suggested story prompts (optional)

2 people

STEPS

1. Each person thinks up a sentence in their head. They can write it down if they wish.

2. The first sentence spoken will be the first sentence of the story. The second sentence spoken will be the last sentence of the story.

3. Invite the children to take turns using their imagination to add another sentence to the story. They get to decide the direction the story will go.

4. Keep going until the second person uses the last sentence they created to end the story.

Modification: Expand the challenge to see if the kids can act out the whole story.

Did you know? Creating and remembering lines while listening to another person requires a lot of brain activity. You must use your abilities to think creatively and listen actively at the same time.

Three-Headed Dragon

It's often said that two heads are better than one. Well, I think three heads are even better! In this activity, three children will work together to create a story—one word at a time—until the 15 minutes are up.

Prep: None

Activity time: 15 minutes

Place: Anywhere

MATERIALS

3 children

Picture cards (optional)

STEPS

1. The 3 children link arms. They are now a three-headed dragon! Their goal is to tell a story 1 word at a time.

2. The first child says the first word, the second child adds on a second word, and the third child adds on a third word.

3. This process continues until the story is complete.

Modification: If needed, they can pick a card to determine what the story will be about. This may help scaffold their creative thinking process.

Sock Puppet Production

Puppets are a timeless way to get into character and tell a story. Think of this as children acting things out with their G.I. Joes or Barbies, except this time with puppets. So the sky's the limit on the kind of characters they can be!

Prep: 5 minutes

Activity time: 30 minutes

Place: Indoors at a solid work surface to make the puppets and behind a couch or table to put on the show

MATERIALS

2 or more old socks

Markers (permanent is best so you can wash the puppets when they get dirty)

Embellishments (yarn for hair, googly eyes, fabric, buttons, etc.)

Hot glue gun

STEPS

1. Announce to your child that you're going to make puppets and put on a show.

2. Take one of the old socks and place it on the hand they do not write with.

3. Invite them to add a mouth, eyes, and any other details they'd like to make it look like their favorite characters. They can use markers and any extra embellishments (see Safety Tip).

4. Once they've made at least two puppets, invite them to plan, rehearse, and act out a play using the puppets, either alone or with others.

Modification: If guidance is needed, give suggestions like: What would a day at the beach be like for these characters? What would happen if they went camping or climbed a mountain?

SAFETY TIP: An adult should operate the hot glue gun. Keep the hot glue gun out of your child's reach.

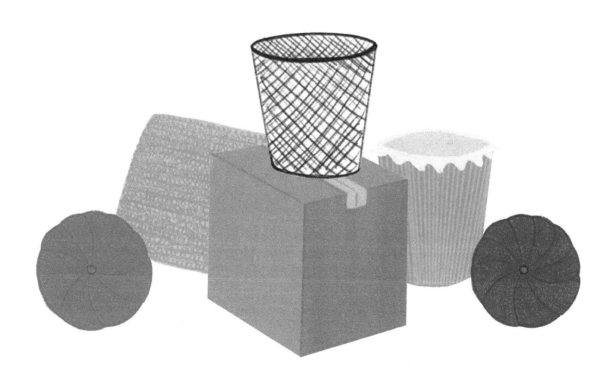

Let's Improvise!

Improvisation is a great life skill and brain builder. This activity allows children to practice thinking on their feet as they create small acting scenes. Watch and see—this promises to be a fun and funny activity for all!

Prep: 5 minutes

Activity time: 15 to 20 minutes

Place: Anywhere

MATERIALS

Suggestion cards (optional)

Props, such as toilet paper tubes, wooden spoons, frying pan, hats, blankets (really anything at all will work!)

STEPS

1. Give the child a subject. For example, lost at sea.

2. Have them pick one of the random items and show how they would use it for the topic. For example, they're on a boat and they grab the frying pan, using it as a paddle to get to shore, or they use toilet paper rolls as binoculars to see where the shore is.

3. This impromptu storytelling can continue for as long as they'd like. Invite them to continue the story with different props. For example, adding the props they would use if they reached land. They can also use props to tell one-line stories for a variety of new subjects.

Modification: Add to the challenge by having them pick their prop with their eyes closed, or you can pick it for them. This way they don't even get to see the item before they must find a creative way to use it in the scenario.

Chapter Five

Let's Create: Collaboration!

Collaborating creatively with others is important for children in this age group—after all, it's building the foundation for the teamwork skills they will use for their entire life. Collaboration allows children to bounce their ideas off others and react to another person's ideas and actions in an open-ended way. Children learn how to work with others cooperatively and compromise and improvise when something doesn't go as planned. This can happen in a home or school setting with peers, siblings, and even adults. Different collaborations will help kids work more seamlessly with others, no matter the setting. This skill will help them become lifelong learners and true team players.

WORKING TOGETHER

No matter what path your child takes in life, collaboration is sure to be a part of it. Their success in relationships, school, career, family, and society will be partly determined by their ability to work as part of a team. Working together is critical—we all share this Earth. But the benefits of collaboration transcend this ability to work together.

The ideas that come from putting many heads together are inevitably more plentiful and diverse than the ideas that sprout from just one brain. But teamwork doesn't just happen. It takes time for a child to understand the concept of listening and accepting others' ideas. Kids want their way, and compromise is a skill they must cultivate by learning empathy and the notion that everyone wants to be heard. It's a tough lesson, especially when different personalities come together. Teams have leaders, followers, doers, and sometimes even slackers—those who aren't one bit interested in the project at hand.

The more practice children get working together with different people and situations, the more innovative, analytical, and broad-thinking they will become. All of the following activities are fun, but they also provide useful opportunities to build skills like thinking and working together as part of a team. Listen in and try to discern what strengths your child brings to the activity table and which parts of working together they may need a little extra help with. Let them have fun with it, knowing they are also learning great skills for life!

Connect the Sounds (116)

Musical Freeze (117)

Appliance Box Castle (118)

Awesome Me, Awesome You (120)

Just Glow With It (122)

Wax It Together (123)

How in the Hoop? (124)

Assembly-Line Art (125)

Glow Rock Hunt (126)

All-Tied-Up Obstacle Course (127)

Connect the Sounds

If your child likes the age-old game of Telephone, let them try this one with some friends, which uses strings of sounds instead of words and phrases. It's good for collaborative skills, but it's also good for some giggles when they hear the end product!

Prep: None

Activity time: 15 to 30 minutes

Place: Anywhere

MATERIALS

3 or more people

STEPS

1. Have everyone sit either in a circle or a straight line. Announce that they are going to play Connect the Sounds.

2. Choose someone to start with a sound. They will quietly make that sound in the second person's ear so that only the second person can hear it.

3. The second person will make the previous sound, then add their sound to it in the third person's ear.

4. One by one, they will have to repeat all previous sounds and their new sounds, too.

5. After the game reaches the final person, that person will make all the sounds they remember out loud.

6. Invite them to repeat this game with a new starting person and new sounds as many times as they would like.

Modification: If the children need guidance, you can give a suggestion, such as animal sounds.

Did you know? Activities like this one increase memory and comprehension skills. The more connections children make, the more being creative comes naturally.

Musical Freeze

Dance is a wonderful creative outlet. Everyone has their own way of doing it. In Musical Freeze, the music maestro will play the music and choose the topic. What topic? Well, when the kids freeze, they will freeze as the topic chosen by the maestro—animals, athletes, soldiers—whatever. This activity will help children relate music to bodily movement and learn to comply with the rules of the music maestro.

Prep: 2 minutes

Activity time: 30 minutes

Place: Anywhere near a music source

MATERIALS

3 or more people, 5 is ideal

Music source

STEPS

1. Tell the children they will be playing Musical Freeze.

2. Choose one child to be the music maestro. They will turn the music on and off. They will also choose a subject, such as animals. When the music starts, the kids dance. When the music stops, they have to freeze, imitating an animal of their choice.

3. Direct the music maestro to turn the music on to start the game. They can turn off the music whenever they wish.

4. If someone doesn't freeze or cannot think of an animal (or whichever topic) to freeze into, they are out of the game. But in the spirit of keeping the creativity flowing, they become the music maestro. Make sure everyone gets a turn!

Did you know? In addition to fostering collaboration, activities like these increase critical-thinking skills, spatial reasoning, and motor skill improvement.

Appliance Box Castle

Building something imaginative out of a large box allows children's creative juices to flow in amazing ways. Invite a friend over for your child to work with. They can draw out their ideas on paper, and then start creating, or skip the paper design and just talk it through. I've provided directions for a castle as one idea, but they can make it anything they'd like. They can use it as their secret clubhouse or add pillows or holiday lights inside and make it a cozy oasis for reading and relaxing.

Prep: 10 minutes

Activity time: 45 minutes

Place: Indoors on the floor or outdoors on a hard surface

MATERIALS

Large appliance box (see Tip)

Black marker

Box cutter or sharp knife (see Safety Tip)

2 (12-inch) pieces of rope (at least ¼ inch thick)

Paint

Paint brushes

2 (5-by-5-inch) square pieces of material (optional)

2 dowels (optional)

Masking or duct tape

STEPS

1. Place a large appliance box on the ground.

2. Invite the children to draw how they would like the top of the castle to be cut out on the box. Cut out along the lines they drew for the top of the castle (see Safety Tip).

3. Next, have the children draw where they would like the door. Let them know it can be curved at the top if they'd like.

4. Cut the outline for the top and sides of the door. Keep the bottom part attached so the door flaps down.

5. Cut two dime-sized holes on the sides of the door and the sides of the box right next to the door. On each side, attach one end of the rope to the hole in the side of the door and the other to the hole in the wall right next to that door.

6. Invite the children to paint anything they'd like on the outside of the castle. Allow to dry.

7. Have them tape a fabric square to one end of each dowel for flags, if desired. They can tape the flags to the top of the castle. The castle is now ready for use!

SAFETY TIP: An adult should cut the box as needed.

Tip: You don't need to buy a new dishwasher to get a big box—just get one from an appliance store!

Did you know? That trademark shape at the top of a castle wall was designed for a specific use. That high-low design provided what were called crenellations, the notches that would allow the castle defenders to have a safe position through which to defend the castle.

Awesome Me, Awesome You

Children love doing activities that involve themselves, but this one will add a collaborative twist as your child invites a friend, sibling, or you to join in by adding their favorite describing words about them. This creative outlet allows them to look at all their unique features and replicate them on paper in their own way and receive a compliment from a friend. This also teaches a child that sharing their creation with others can be fun. The self-portrait can be realistic or even abstract; either way, self-portraits are great for self-esteem.

Prep: None

Activity time: 30 to 40 minutes

Place: Indoors at a solid work surface

MATERIALS

Mirror

Paper

Pencil

Markers

Friend, sibling, or other family member

STEPS

1. Tell your child that they will create a self-portrait and incorporate words others use to describe them.

2. Have your child look in the mirror. They can describe their features first to help guide them into drawing them easily.

3. Have them begin with any feature, such as their head, and continue onto the others—eyes, eyebrows, nose, mouth, freckles, you name it—until all features are drawn. Leave some space on the page for others to add words of praise.

4. Invite your child to color their self-portrait in non-traditional colors and ways. This allows them to get a bit more creative and flexible with their portrait.

5. Finally, invite your child to show their portrait and ask around for describing words. They can ask you, siblings, friends, Grandma—for words that describe them. Hopefully somebody says ARTISTIC! and CREATIVE! They can add these words to the paper if they want or invite you or their siblings to write the words in the white space around the portrait.

Modification: If your child does not want anyone writing on their paper, they can simply ask people to offer describing words about them and write them down themselves. For older or more skilled kids, allow them to use shapes and pieces to create a more abstract self-portrait; even making it a little Picasso-like!

Did you know? Vincent Van Gogh created amazing self-portraits among his many other works. It is said that he only sold one painting during his lifetime. He had a creative soul and eye for detail, yet it wasn't truly appreciated by the public until after his passing.

Just Glow With It

Glow party time! What kid doesn't like to create forts out of their blankets, read with flashlights, and dance in the dark? Just Glow With It mixes dance party with the dark. It will be a glowing good time, and everyone gets a turn deciding what activity to do with the glow sticks in the dark.

Prep: 5 to 10 minutes

Activity time: 20 to 30 minutes

Place: Indoors or outdoors in the dark

MATERIALS

3 or more people

Paper

Pens

Jar

Glow necklaces (at least 1 per person)

Glow bracelets (at least 1 per person)

Glow-in-the-dark washable paint (optional)

Music

STEPS

1. Invite the children to write down an activity they'd like to do at the glow party. Suggestions might include a tent party, glow stick hide-and-seek, glow freeze dance, glow follow the leader, glow toss, etc. Place all the suggestions in a jar.

2. Invite all the kids to put on the glow bracelets, necklaces, and even paint if desired.

3. Turn off the lights and turn on the music.

4. Take turns pulling ideas from the jar. Finish things off with a freestyle dance party, where the kids dance any way they'd like with the glow accessories.

Wax It Together

This project combines wax, creativity, and amazing art masterpieces created by adult and child collaboration.

Prep: 5 minutes

Activity time: 20 minutes

Place: Indoors at a solid work surface near an electrical outlet

MATERIALS

Different colored crayons

Paper

1 sheet of wax paper per piece of art (wax paper should be about the same size as the artwork)

Iron (see Safety Tip)

Vegetable peeler or cheese grater with a handle (see Safety Tip)

2 or more people, including one adult

STEPS

1. Together with your child(ren), choose the colors you want for your artwork.

2. Use the grater or peeler to shred specks of crayon for your child (see safety tip). Make a small pile of each color.

3. Take turns adding specks of crayons to a piece of paper. Work together to create your collaborative artwork in any pattern you'd like.

4. Once you've put all the colors you'd like on your collaborative artwork, place the wax paper on top of the paper.

5. Have an adult plug in the iron, then iron the wax paper. This will melt and transfer the wax to the drawing paper.

6. Once cooled, peel the wax paper off to reveal the finished art piece. Discuss what was fun and challenging about working together on this collaborative project.

SAFETY TIP: Keep the iron out of children's reach. Only allow a capable older child to use a grater or peeler, and make sure they keep their fingers a safe distance from the blades.

How in the Hoop?

Let your child get together with their most curious, outside-the-box, problem-solving friends and try their collective hand at Hula-Hoop navigation. This is one of many collaborative activities children can do with Hula-Hoops. It will require teamwork and some creative thinking to complete.

Prep: None

Activity time: Up to 30 minutes

Place: Indoors or outdoors in an open area

MATERIALS

6 or more people

1 Hula-Hoop

STEPS

1. Have the children hold hands together in a circle.

2. Let the Hula-Hoop rest looped on the wrists of one set of participants.

3. Without letting go of the others' hands, tell the children they need to figure out how to move the Hula-Hoop from the first person all the way around the circle to the last person.

4. Encourage the kids to discuss as a team some ways that they can transfer the Hula-Hoop without letting go. Remind them to listen to each others' ideas and try multiple ways to see which one works best.

Did you know? Trying different strategies to accomplish something is a great way to exercise the brain.

Assembly-Line Art

This drawing activity requires children to work together, take turns, and even compromise, as children will have differing viewpoints about what they want to create. It'll also require some improvisational drawing and thinking skills—all great skills for life.

Prep time: 5 minutes

Activity time: 15 to 20 minutes

Place: Indoors or outdoors at a solid work surface

MATERIALS

2 to 4 people

Pen, pencil, or markers

Drawing paper

STEPS

1. Announce to the children that they are going to create a piece of art together.

2. One child will start by drawing a line or shape.

3. The next child will add onto the first line or shape to create something new.

4. Everyone will take turns and add to the picture until they're satisfied they have finished their creation.

Modification: For older children, suggest that the person drawing be blindfolded or keep their eyes closed as the person to their left guides them with words on where to draw.

Glow Rock Hunt

Painting rocks has gained momentum in the past few years, but this activity takes it to the next level with glow-in-the-dark paint and a fun collaborative rock hunt! This activity is great for kids who love to draw and paint and for kids that love to go hunting for things. It gives children a chance to make creative designs on the rocks and place the rocks in interesting places for others to find.

Prep: 10 minutes

Activity time: 50 minutes to 1 hour

Place: Outdoors or indoors on a solid work surface, then in the dark

MATERIALS

10 or more rocks

Newspaper

Glow-in-the-dark paint

Paintbrushes

3 or more people

STEPS

1. Wash the rocks to remove any dirt, then dry them.

2. Cover a work surface with newspaper. Paint the rocks. Decorate with artsy designs, and allow them to sit in the sun to dry and soak up the light.

3. Once nighttime falls, have one person hide all the rocks, indoors or out.

4. The remaining people will hunt for all the rocks.

Modification: For younger kids, have each paint their rocks with one specific color and have someone else hide their color rocks. When it gets dark, they can hunt for their own rocks. For older kids, let them create a riddle or clue that will lead others to their rock. This puts a little bit of critical-thinking skills in the mix and helps them think creatively.

All-Tied-Up Obstacle Course

Obstacle courses are lots of fun, but this one will test your child's teamwork skills as they work in pairs, tied together, to complete a course they've designed—go team!

Prep: 10 minutes

Activity time: 20 minutes

Place: Anywhere indoors or out—even at a park

MATERIALS

Items to climb on, around, over, or under (chairs, stumps, cones, leaf piles, etc.)

Scarf or rope

6 or more people (ideally at least 3 teams of 2)

STEPS

1. Let your child and a friend work together to set up their obstacle course. Encourage them to include climbing, curves, and twists to make the course more challenging to navigate. You can assist them with building the course or coming up with ideas.

2. Have each child stand next to a partner.

3. Tie the scarf around each pair's inside legs.

4. Time each pair as they navigate the course together. Encourage them because it will take teamwork and some creative moves to get through the course.

Resources

These are some great resources to use to get a child's creative juices flowing in the classroom or at home!

BOOKS

Books are a priceless resource. The following are books that teach children it's okay not to be perfect, to make mistakes, and to try new things. These stories will help them become more willing to try new, creative things without fear of failure or judgment. They work great alongside the activities in this book. I know this, because these are staple books I use in my classroom, too!

I Can't Do That, YET: Growth Mindset by Esther Cordova and Maima W. Adiputri. **This book is all about having a growth mindset and encourages the child to stay positive and keep trying new things.**

Beautiful Oops! by Barney Saltzberg. **This book teaches children that mistakes can become something beautiful.**

The Dot by Peter H. Reynolds. **This book is the charming tale of a child that discovers her artistic talent.**

The Girl Who Never Made Mistakes by Mark Pett and Gary Rubinstein. **A story that shows it's more fun to enjoy and learn from your mistakes than to try to be perfect.**

Giraffes Can't Dance by Giles Andreae. **This book can be read before any of the dance activities to promote self-confidence.**

Scribble Stones by Diane Alber. **This book would be great to read for the Glow Rock Hunt activity (page 126).**

I'm Not Just a Scribble . . . **or** *Splatter* by Diane Alber. **These two books would be great to read before any of the activities that involve drawing a picture, emoting feelings, problem-solving, or teamwork.**

WEBSITES

Posterini.com. **This website allows children to create things like posters with pictures/graphics.**

Readwritethink.com. **This website has a poster making feature and also allows children to write stories and make pamphlets with photos.**

Ccteachfirst.blogspot.com. **This website offers free, printable journal writing/handwriting paper.**

Artsandculture.google.com. **If you do not have a local museum, Google Arts and Culture is a fun way to expose children to new cultures and artwork.**

AROUND TOWN

Craft stores. **Some local craft or hardware stores have free classes for kids to create or complete a fun project.**

Local museums. **This is a great way to allow children to experience different types of art, from traditional to abstract, as well as other creations and inventions throughout history. Many museums also have a hands-on creating section. Check with your local museums to see if they offer free admission on select days.**

Kiln/pottery shops. **See if your town has a local pottery activity center. Kids can create their own pottery and paint it there, leaving with a ready-to-use product.**

REFERENCES

Alban, Deane and Patrick Alban. "How Music Affects the Brain." Be Brain Fit. Last modified January 7, 2018. https://bebrainfit.com/music-brain/

"American Academy of Pediatrics Announces New Recommendations for Children's Media Use." American Academy of Pediatrics, Accessed April 5, 2017. https://www.aap.org/en-us/about-the-aap/aap-press-room/pages/american -academy-of-pediatrics-announces-new-recommendations-for-childrens -media-use.aspx

Brenner, Grant Hilary, MD, FAPA. "Your Brain on Creativity." Psychology Today. Last Modified February 22, 2018. https://www.psychologytoday.com/us/blog /experimentations/201802/your-brain-creativity

Child First. "Executive Functioning." https://www.childfirst.org/our-work /home-based-intervention/executive-functioning

"Dancing Can Reverse the Signs of Aging in the Brain." *Frontiers in Human Neuroscience* (2017). https://medicalxpress.com/news/2017-08-reverse -aging-brain.html

"Executive Function and Self-Regulation." *Harvard University Center on the Developing Child.* https://developingchild.harvard.edu/science/key-concepts /executive-function/

Mayo Clinic Staff. "Screen Time and Children: How to Guide Your Child." *Mayo Clinic.* Last modified June 20, 2019. https://www.mayoclinic.org/healthy-lifestyle /childrens-health/in-depth/screen-time/art-20047952

Michaelis, Ben, Ph. D., "Why Nurturing Creativity in Kids Is So Important." *Exquisite Minds.* https://www.exquisite-minds.com/idea-of-the-week /why-nurturing-creativity-is-important/

Mind Tools Team. "Creative Problem Solving: Finding Innovative Solutions to Challenges." *Mind Tools.* https://www.mindtools.com/pages/article/creative -problem-solving.htm

Nemours Children's Health System. "Limit Use of TV, Computers, and Mobile Devices" https://healthykidshealthyfuture.org/5-healthy-goals/reduce -screen-time/

Nicoloff, Françoise. "5 Reasons Why Screen Time Is Bad for Young Children." *Mindd Foundation.* https://mindd.org/screen-time/

Ricci, Mary Cay. *Mindsets in the Classroom: Building a Growth Mindset Learning Community.* Waco, TX: Prufrock Press, 2017.

INDEX

ABOUT THE AUTHOR

Trisha Riché is a former nanny with over 20 years of experience as a tutor in art and academics. For the past 15 years, she has worked as an elementary school teacher, where she uses her background in visual arts and creativity daily in her classroom. She likes llamas, loves Halloween, and enjoys creating crafts.

Getting people excited and involved in creative activities like the ones in this book is her passion. Riché wrote a blog on creativity for Edutopia and presented a class on harnessing creativity in the classroom at the national Staff Development for Educators conference. She was also nominated and selected as a finalist in the Great American Teach-Off in 2011 and chosen as Teacher of the Year in 2016. Riché lives in Florida with her bearded dragon Puff, but Louisiana will always be her home.

CPSIA information can be obtained
at www.ICGtesting.com
Printed in the USA
LVHW071610070220
646024LV00004B/9